Copyright © 1990 Modern Publishing, a division of Unisystems, Inc.

Copyright © Aladdin Books Ltd.

Originally designed and produced as First Sight Books by Aladdin Books Ltd., 28 Percy Street, London, WIP 9FF

First published in Great Britain in 1987, 1988, 1989 by Franklin Watts 96 Leonard St., London EC2A 4RH

Birds of Prey

Design by David West, Children's Book Design
Illustrations by Louise Nevett and Tessa Barwick
Picture research by Cecilia Weston-Baker
Consultant, Dr. Phillip JK Burton

Gorillas and Chimpanzees

Design by David West, Children's Book Design
Illustrations by Louise Nevett and Tessa Barwick
Picture research by Cecilia Weston-Baker
Edited by Kate Petty

Lions and Tigers

Design by David West, Children's Book Design
Illustrations by Tessa Barwick
Picture research by Cecilia Weston-Baker
Edited by Denny Robson
Consultant, John Stidworthy

Poisonous Insects

Design by David West, Children's Book Design
Illustrations by George Thompson
Picture research by Cecilia Weston-Baker
Edited by Denny Robson
Consultant, John Stidworthy

Creatures of the Deep

Design by David West, Children's Book Design
Illustrations by Aziz Khan
Picture research by Cecilia Weston-Baker
Edited by Scott Steedman
Consultant, Miles Barton

Pythons and Boas

Design by David West, Children's Book Design
Illustrations by Alan Male
Picture research by Cecilia Weston-Baker
Edited by Denny Robson
Consultant, John Stidworthy

™ World of Wildlife is a trademark owned by Modern Publishing, a division of Unisystems, Inc.

® Honey Bear Books is a trademark owned by Honey Bear Productions, Inc., and is registered in the U.S. Patent and Trademark Office.

Printed in Colombia

FASCINATING ANIMALS

Modern Publishing
A Division of Unisystems, Inc.
New York, New York 10022

CONTENTS

INTRODUCTION

From our closest primate relatives to the bizarre creatures that swim in the cold, dark depths of the ocean three miles down, life on Earth is made up of an infinite variety of animals. There are over a million different species of insects alone! *Fascinating Animals* provides just a glimpse into the wonderful richness of nature.

Learn all about birds of prey, gorillas and chimpanzees, lions and tigers, poisonous insects, creatures of the deep, and pythons and boas—what they eat, where they live and how they survive in today's changing world. Each chapter contains many full-color photographs and drawings, a Spotters' Guide or Identification Chart to help you recognize the animals at the zoo or in the wild, and a game or activity that applies the information you have learned. Each page contains fascinating facts about these animals, and a Survival Guide included in every chapter tells you the ways in which each animal is threatened by changes in the natural world.

The life of each and every animal is a complex strategy for survival that has evolved over millions of years by adaptation to different environments and this strategy continues today.

Prepare for a wonderful journey as you begin an excursion into the fascinating World of Wildlife.

The little square shows you the size of the bird. Each side represents about 3.3 feet.

A red square means that a bird is in need of protection. Turn to the Survival File.

The picture opposite is of a Snowy Owl from the Arctic Circle

Chapter 1

BIRDS OF PREY

Kate Petty

Facts to Know

Eagles, hawks, falcons, vultures, owls—these are all
birds of prey, or "raptors," as they are sometimes
called. Most of them are large birds with hooked beaks
and long, sharp talons. They need these to hunt
and kill other birds and animals for their food.

Like many wild animals today, birds of prey are at risk
from changes in the environment. The forests they live
in are cut down, or the rivers they fish from are
polluted. Thirty years ago some birds of prey nearly
became extinct. Many were shot and trapped. Others
were poisoned by pesticides. Now people are doing
what they can to protect them and make sure that they
are still around for you and your own children to see.

◁ **Bald Eagle, no longer a common bird of prey**

Birds you might see

A Buzzard soaring above the fields is quite a common sight in Europe. So is its cousin, the Red-tailed Hawk, in the United States.

If you see any large bird soaring, hovering or swooping, it could be a bird of prey. It might be a Kestrel hovering in the air close to a highway. Or you might spot a Sparrowhawk skimming the treetops, making all the smaller birds call out in alarm.

Birdwatchers learn to recognize birds of prey from a distance by the shape of their wings and tail feathers. You will need a pair of binoculars to get a good look at their colors and markings. Then you can use the Spotters' Guide to help you identify the birds

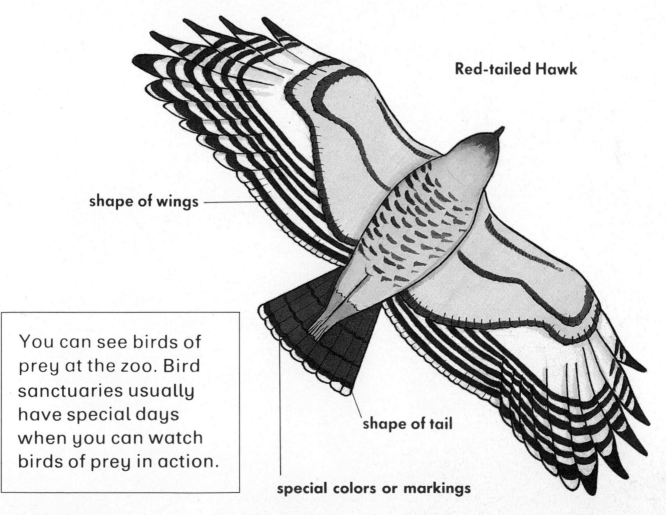

Red-tailed Hawk

shape of wings —

shape of tail

special colors or markings

You can see birds of prey at the zoo. Bird sanctuaries usually have special days when you can watch birds of prey in action.

◁ **Common Buzzard with its kill**

Keen sight

All hunting birds need excellent eyesight for spotting their prey from a long way off. Some of them use a favorite rock or perch as a lookout point. A Kestrel hovers in the air when it is searching for food. It scans the field below with a steady gaze and then swoops down on its victim. It can see a grasshopper in the grass from 330 feet away.

Birds of prey have big eyes, which are often brightly colored. The Black-shouldered Kite has beautiful coral-red eyes. They are protected from the sun by feathery "eyebrows."

Both these birds are looking at you! Birds of prey look separately out of each eye to see sideways but they use both eyes together to see straight ahead.

Black-shouldered Kite

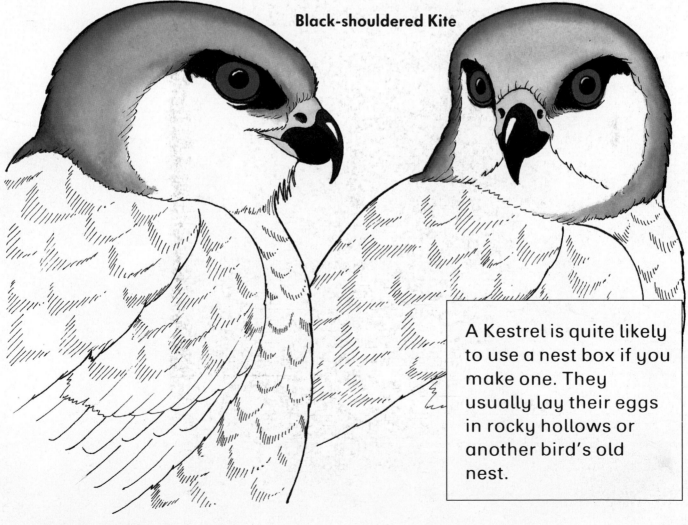

A Kestrel is quite likely to use a nest box if you make one. They usually lay their eggs in rocky hollows or another bird's old nest.

◁ **Old World Kestrel hovering**

Talons that kill

Most birds of prey use their feet to grab and kill their victims. Each foot has four toes with long, curved claws called talons. The three forward-pointing toes are for grasping. The talon on the back toe is like a knife that stabs the prey.

The long middle toe of the Sparrowhawk helps it to snatch little birds in midair. The Osprey lives on fish. Its feet are specially adapted for fishing, with two toes pointing forwards and two pointing backwards. The undersides of the toes are covered in tiny sharp spikes, called spicules, for gripping slithery fish. The powerful grasp of the Harpy Eagle's claws can crush a monkey or a sloth in a very few seconds.

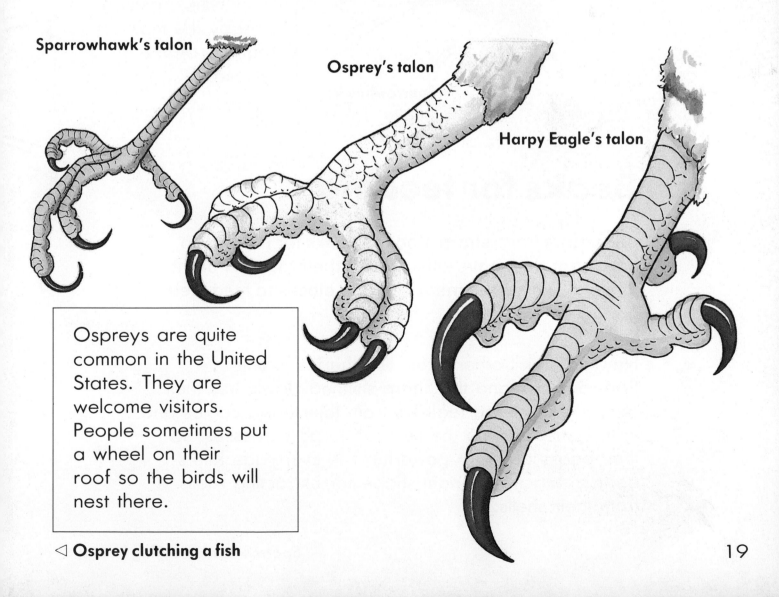

Sparrowhawk's talon

Osprey's talon

Harpy Eagle's talon

Ospreys are quite common in the United States. They are welcome visitors. People sometimes put a wheel on their roof so the birds will nest there.

◁ **Osprey clutching a fish**

Everglade Kite

White-headed African Vulture

Sparrowhawk

Sparrowhawks take their prey to a regular plucking post. You can recognize a plucking post by the mass of feathers on the ground.

Beaks for feeding

All raptors have sharp, hooked beaks for tearing up prey after they have killed it with their talons. Parent birds will shred the meat into tiny pieces to feed their young.

Hawks that kill other birds, like the fierce little Sparrowhawk and the Sharp-shinned Hawk, use their beaks to pluck the feathers from their prey. Eagles and vultures need to rip the flesh off large carcasses, so their beaks are very powerful. The Everglade Kite's beak is exactly the right shape for extracting snails from their shells.

Sparrowhawk plucking its prey ▷

On the wing

The shape of a bird's wings tells you something about the way it flies. Eagles and vultures have long wings to soar on currents of warm air called thermals. Like many falcons, Kestrels have pointed wings for fast flying. They can beat their wings rapidly to hover as well. Woodland birds of prey like the Forest Falcon have more rounded wings for flying among the trees.

In spring some birds put on a wonderful show of aerobatics. When Montagu's Harrier is showing off to his mate he swoops and somersaults, climbs and dives again. Then the female joins in, rolling over as she flies to take a piece of food offered by her mate. Harriers are long-distance fliers, sometimes covering 150 miles a day on their way to warmer countries.

Black Vulture

Kestrel

Forest Falcon

Migrating birds often become exhausted. This makes them easy targets for bird-hunters in countries where birds are not protected by law.

◁ **Montagu's Harrier, a long-distance flier**

23

◁ **Peregrine Falcon in its natural habitat**

People have kept falcons as hunting birds for thousands of years. The falcon is trained to return to its owner, who wears a special glove for it to perch on.

The victim is sighted . . .

the falcon goes into the stoop . . .

reaching speeds of 125mph . . .

the victim is killed with a blow from the hind toe.

The streamlined hunter

The Peregrine Falcon's spectacular steep dive for its prey is called a "stoop." Once common all over the world, the Peregrine Falcon almost completely disappeared in some places about thirty years ago. The Peregrine feeds off smaller birds. These little birds were eating grain that had been sprayed with pesticide. The poison built up inside the falcons. It stopped their eggs from forming properly, so the Peregrines almost died out. There aren't as many poisonous pesticides now, and Peregrines are slowly becoming more common again.

25

The silent hunters

Owls hunt at night, so they need to see in the dark. They also have excellent hearing and special soft feathers for silent flight.

There are 140 different kinds of owls in the world. Small owls, like the Little Owl, are no bigger than 8 inches. The biggest, the Eagle Owl, is about 27 inches long.

Barn Owls were once found on farms all over Europe and America. They were useful to farmers because they killed rats. Now many of their homes, particularly in old barns and elm trees, have been destroyed.

Birds of prey can't easily digest bones and feathers, so they bring these up again in a tight little ball called a pellet. You can often tell what an owl has eaten by examining one of its pellets.

Large owls eat all these creatures. They will sometimes swallow them whole.

owl pellets

rabbits

frogs

grasshoppers

field voles

mice

moles

26

Barn Owl hunting in the snow ▷

Nesting

This Golden Eagle and her mate come back to the same nest year after year. Their nest is called an aerie. It is made of twigs and lined with leaves. They build it high up where no harm can come to the eggs. The eagle is a fierce hunter but a gentle mother. She sits on the eggs for six weeks before they hatch. The chicks learn to fly when they are twelve weeks old, but both parents still feed them for many weeks after that.

Some birds that fly and hunt low down build their nests on the ground. Marsh Harriers make their nests in the reeds. The male feeds the female when she is sitting on the eggs. She flies off the nest and rolls over in the air to take the food from him.

◁ **Marsh Harrier with its young**

The eggs of most birds of prey are white speckled with brown. NEVER, EVER steal eggs from a nest or disturb nesting birds. You could be breaking the law.

◁ **Golden Eagle with its young**

The majestic eagles

Eagles are the largest and most powerful birds of prey.
Compare them with others in the Spotters' Guide.
Many of them are over 27 inches long with a wingspan of
over 6.5 feet. The Harpy Eagle from the South
American jungle is the largest of all. The biggest one
recorded weighed over 26 pounds. It preys on
monkeys, oppossums and macaws.

People all over the world have used the eagle as a
symbol of strength and power. The Bald Eagle is the
national emblem of the USA, though today it is a rare
bird found mostly in Alaska.

Eagles can kill animals
that are much bigger
than themselves. They
are sometimes
responsible for killing
sheep. More often they
prey on smaller
creatures that they can
carry off.

**The flag of the President of the
United States shows a Bald Eagle**

Rare Harpy Eagle from the South American jungle ▷

Nature's cleaners

Vultures do not usually kill for their food. They feed off "carrion"—the flesh of dead animals. Most vultures live in hot, wild places. The White-backed Vulture lives in Asia. The King Vulture is quite common in Central and South America. They soar on the rising hot air and fly high, searching for dead or dying animals. They do a useful job by eating carrion that would otherwise rot in the hot sun. Their heads and necks are bald so they can thrust them deep into the carcasses.

Condors are vultures. The Andean Condor is the largest of all vultures. The California Condor from North America is sadly now almost extinct.

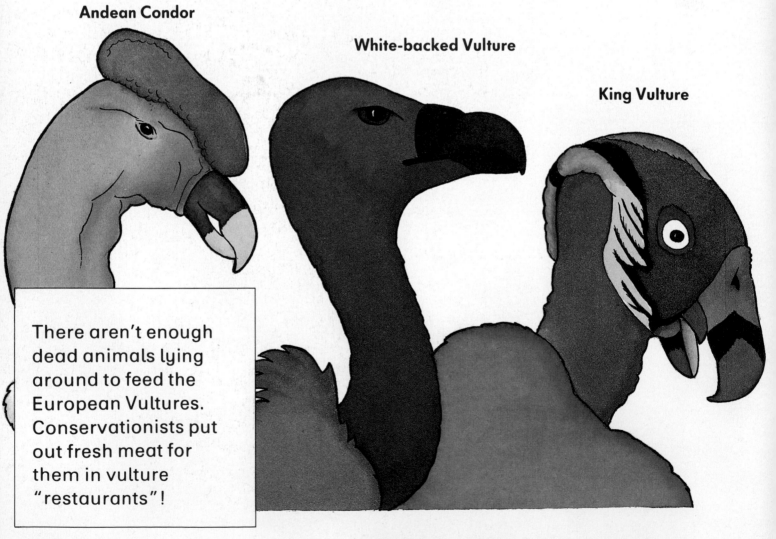

Andean Condor

White-backed Vulture

King Vulture

There aren't enough dead animals lying around to feed the European Vultures. Conservationists put out fresh meat for them in vulture "restaurants"!

One of the few remaining California Condors ▷

Unusual birds of prey

The Secretary Bird lives in the African grasslands. It runs on its long legs more often than it flies. As well as insects and small mammals the Secretary Bird eats tortoises and snakes. It kicks them to death with its large feet. This one has caught a frog. It is called a Secretary Bird after the secretaries of 200 years ago, when men wore wigs. Secretaries stuck their quill pens in their wigs for safe keeping!

The African Harrier Hawk has legs which bend both ways. It searches all round a hole in a tree trunk with its foot. It can grab a bat from the top of the hole or a baby bird from the bottom.

African Harrier Hawk

Secretary Birds are sometimes kept in captivity in South Africa to keep down snakes and rats.

◁ **Secretary Bird demolishing a frog**

Survival file

Many birds of prey must struggle to survive in our changing world. Like all animals, they suffer when their habitat is destroyed or altered. Many farmers and gamekeepers think they are pests and try to get rid of them. More and more people use cars, which bring hikers and photographers tramping closer than ever to their hidden homes.

Young male Sparrowhawk caught in a pole trap

So many Ospreys were killed in Britain that there were none left. Now a few pairs have arrived from Scandinavia. Their closely guarded nests are kept secret so they can breed in peace.

The Everglade Kite eats one thing – apple snails. Changes in the countryside made the snail scarce, so feeding refuges have been built for the birds in places where there are still plenty of snails for them.

Male Everglade Kite

You now need a licence to keep a Peregrine Falcon in Britain. Twenty years ago in eastern America the Peregrine Falcon disappeared altogether. Now they are being bred in captivity.

Barn Owls lose their hunting grounds and nesting sites when trees are cut down and old farm buildings are modernised. Nest boxes built near their old nesting sites are bringing some of them back.

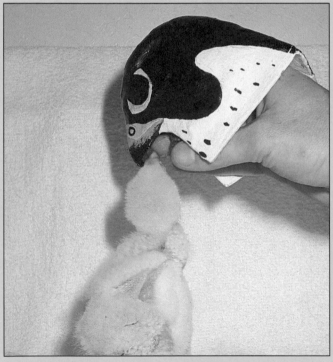

Peregrine chick being hand-fed by "parent"

Montagu's Harrier likes to nest in cornfields. Farmers can help conservationists to protect the birds by not spraying their nesting sites and by waiting for the chicks to grow before cutting the crops.

Golden Eagles were persecuted by farmers and gamekeepers and egg collectors robbed their nests. Now it is illegal to harm a Golden Eagle or go near its nest.

There are only five California Condors left in the wild. Conservationists have made refuges for them and feed them fresh meat. Now they are trying to rear chicks in captivity.

Spotters' guide

This chart shows the birds of prey you are most likely to see in Europe and America. The birds are drawn to scale to show their comparative sizes.

● Europe
◐ N. America
○ S. America

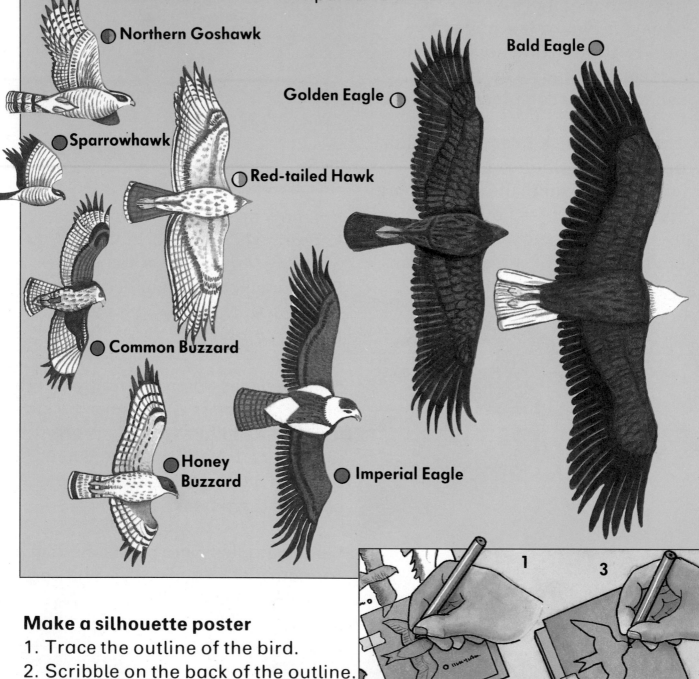

Northern Goshawk

Bald Eagle

Golden Eagle

Sparrowhawk

Red-tailed Hawk

Common Buzzard

Honey Buzzard

Imperial Eagle

Make a silhouette poster
1. Trace the outline of the bird.
2. Scribble on the back of the outline.
3. Lay the tracing the right way up on white paper and go over the outline.
4. Now you have an outline of a bird.
5. Fill in the outline with black.
6. Cut the bird out and stick it onto your poster.

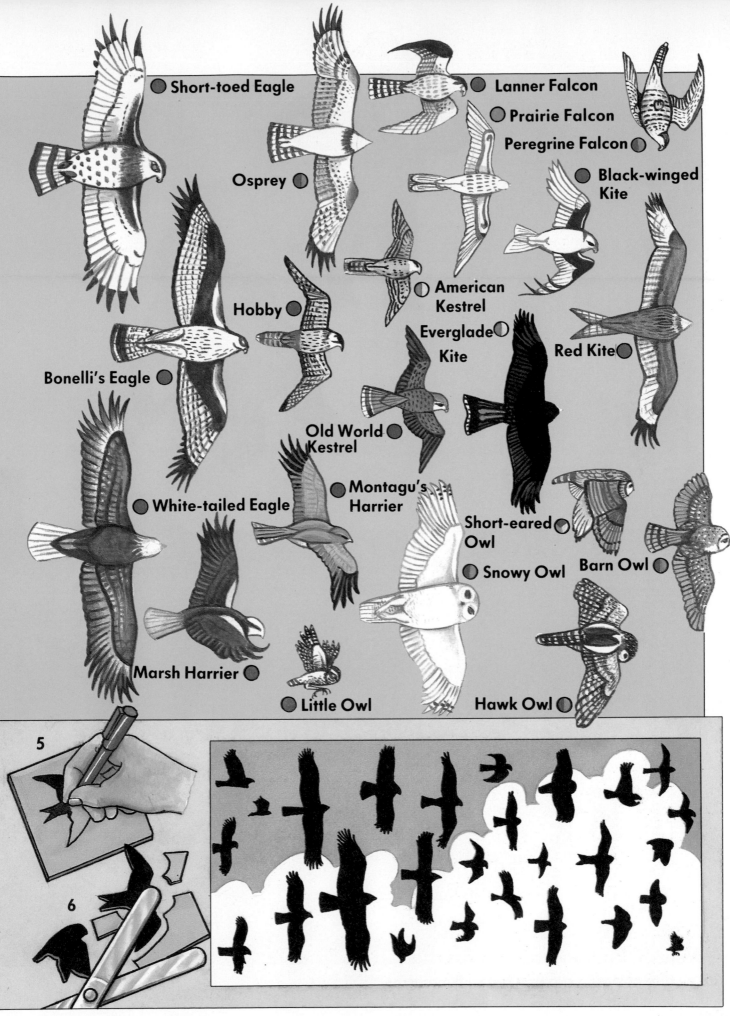

Short-toed Eagle

Lanner Falcon

Prairie Falcon

Peregrine Falcon

Osprey

Black-winged
Kite

Hobby

American
Kestrel

Everglade
Kite

Red Kite

Bonelli's Eagle

Old World
Kestrel

White-tailed Eagle

Montagu's
Harrier

Short-eared
Owl

Snowy Owl

Barn Owl

Marsh Harrier

Little Owl

Hawk Owl

5

6

The little square shows
you the size of the ape compared
with a man. Each side represents
about 5.75 feet.

The picture opposite shows a baby chimpanzee

Chapter 2
GORILLAS
AND
CHIMPANZEES

David Chivers

Facts to Know

Apes, monkeys and humans all belong to the same order of animals, called primates. Gorillas and chimpanzees belong to the ape family, which also includes orangutans and gibbons.

Gorillas and chimpanzees are found only in Africa. There is one kind of gorilla, which is found in West Africa, eastern Zaire, and the mountains of the Rift Valley. There are two kinds of chimpanzee. The pygmy chimpanzee lives south of the Zaire River. The common chimpanzee is found in the far west, center and east of Africa. Both gorillas and chimpanzees are seriously threatened by the clearance of the tropical forests that are their homes.

◁ **Portrait of a gorilla leader**

Life in the trees

Gorillas and chimpanzees are well suited to life in the trees. They are good at climbing and swinging and hanging. Their very long arms are useful for reaching food at the ends of branches. They can grasp with their feet as well as their hands. Like us, they have "opposable" thumbs for grasping and picking. Chimpanzees have "opposable" toes as well.

Male chimpanzees weigh 90 pounds, but male gorillas weigh 350 pounds (twice the weight of an average human). Gorillas are so large that they have to spend a lot of time on the ground. Chimpanzees and gorillas mostly travel by knuckle-walking on all fours, with the hands clenched in a fist and the feet curled up.

human　　　　**chimpanzee**

hands

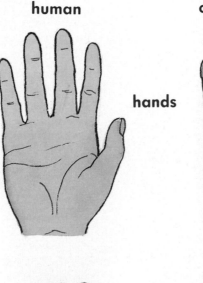 

feet

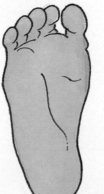 

Chimpanzees are more at home in the trees than gorillas. They sometimes travel short distances by swinging from branch to branch.

◁ **Young mountain gorillas in Rwanda**

45

Eating to live

Although they are so big, gorillas eat mainly leaves. They need to spend most of their time eating. One of their favorite foods is wild celery. A gorilla skull shows that the teeth are big and the jaws are very strong for chewing.

Chimpanzees have a more varied diet. They eat mainly fruit and some leaves, but they are not completely vegetarian like the gorillas. They also eat ants, termites and other insects. Some chimpanzees even eat monkeys, young pigs and antelopes. Chimpanzees have smaller teeth than gorillas. The pointed canine teeth are sometimes used for fighting, but they are good for opening fruit and shredding stems.

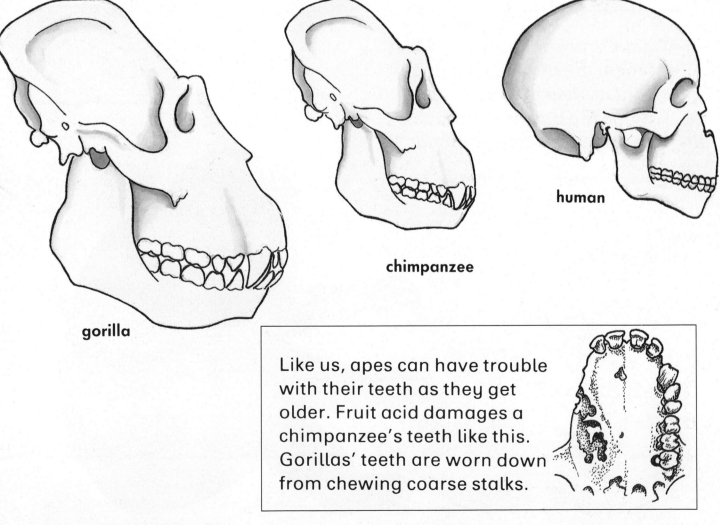

gorilla

chimpanzee

human

Like us, apes can have trouble with their teeth as they get older. Fruit acid damages a chimpanzee's teeth like this. Gorillas' teeth are worn down from chewing coarse stalks.

◁ **Male lowland gorilla eating**

Gathering food

A gorilla group looks for food together. They eat a little and then they move on. There are always plenty of leaves for them to eat. Some groups find fruit to eat as well.

Chimpanzees look for food separately or in small parties. Most of the time they pick fruit and nuts from trees. (In West Africa they can cause problems when they raid plantations.) They eat blossoms and bark from trees, too. Sometimes they peel sticks to "fish" for ants in ant nests or termites in their mounds. They poke the stick into the mound and pull it out covered with the insects. Several chimpanzees will hunt together for monkeys or other animals.

Chimpanzees can't swim. Most of them are afraid of water and avoid it when they can. A few groups are braver and wade into shallow waters for food.

"Fishing" for termites with a stick

Chimpanzee carrying fruit ▷

The gorilla group

Gorillas live in well organized groups. These consist of one adult male, several adult females and their young. There are usually between five and twenty animals altogether. The fur on the adult male turns a silvery white, so he is known as a "silverback." He is the leader of the group and the center of group life. The females gather around him to groom during the midday rest period. He has a remarkable display to scare away other males and to attract females to join his group. He beats his chest with his fists, hoots, barks and roars and then tears up vegetation and dashes from side to side. This display has led people to think that gorillas are ferocious animals. Really they are very gentle creatures.

Jambo, a male silverback, proved how gentle gorillas can be when a small boy fell into his pit at Jersey Zoo. He sat by the injured boy until he woke up, then moved away for keepers to come to the rescue.

Showing them who's boss – leadership display

50   **hooting**   **pretending to feed**   **throwing sticks**

△ **Mountain gorilla beating his chest**

chest beating   **running sideways**   **ground thumping**

51

Chimpanzee society

Chimpanzees live in groups of up to a hundred animals. The group travels around over an area of 4 to 20 square miles. Males often travel together, patrolling the borders of the home range. Sometimes there is fierce fighting between neighboring groups. The females and their young usually search for food separately.

Both male and female chimpanzees are organized so that each animal knows its place. There are several important males in each group, rather than just one leader. Chimpanzees spend many hours grooming one another. This helps to keep them clean but it also strengthens the friendships between them.

hooting – a call to eat

friends hold hands

grooming

The important males in a group of chimpanzees are usually the noisiest and most violent.

◁ **Female chimpanzees grooming each other**

Building a nest

Chimpanzees build nests high up in trees to sleep in at night. First they bend some branches across to make a platform. Then they make a "mattress" out of leaves and mosses. Babies sleep with their mothers. Chimpanzees build a new nest every night. It takes them less than five minutes.

Big gorillas are too heavy to sleep in the trees. They make their nests out of branches and leaves on the ground. A lining of dry dung keeps them warm during the cold nights in the mountains.

Young chimpanzees and gorillas learn how to build nests by watching the older ones. They play at making nests from a very young age.

Gorillas and chimpanzees which have been brought up in cages never learn how to build nests. If they are taken back to the forest they don't know what to do.

Chimpanzee building a bed in the trees

Growing up

A baby gorilla or chimpanzee is born helpless. It clings to its mother's belly all the time. By the age of six months the baby can ride on its mother's back. When it is two it stops feeding on the mother's milk and learns how to eat like an adult. At four it can travel about on its own, but it will stay close to the mother until it is six years old. By then the mother might have another baby. Babies are born only every five or six years.

Like humans, they take a long time to grow up. There is much to learn, mostly from the mother. She spends time playing with the baby as well as teaching it to look after itself. Other group members, even the adult males, are usually very helpful with the little ones.

Chimpanzees in the wild can live for more than 40 years. In zoos they have lived to be over 50.

Mother chimpanzee playing with her baby

◁ **Baby pygmy chimpanzee clinging to its mother**

Showing how they feel

Chimpanzees have very expressive faces. Other chimpanzees can see what they are feeling, whether it is excitement, fear, anger – even joy and sadness.

Chimpanzees call to one another in a great variety of grunts and hoots which almost make a language. Smell and touch are also important in relationships between apes.

Scientists working with chimpanzees have come to understand the way apes communicate with each other. Their expressions are not like ours. For example, when a chimpanzee bares its teeth in a "smile" it is showing fear, not happiness.

sad

fearful

As well as grooming each other, chimpanzee friends hold hands and hug when they meet.

playful

excited

Chimpanzee sticking out its tongue ▷

Special intelligence

Gorillas and chimpanzees have large brains. They find inventive ways to solve problems. Chimpanzees use rocks and twigs as "tools" to help them eat. They use leaves in all sorts of ways — for soaking up water and mopping up food, and even for dabbing at wounds. Chimpanzees also make weapons from sticks and stones to scare off other animals, such as baboons, if they try to steal their food.

Chimpanzees and gorillas have been studied in homes and zoos. Some have been shown how to paint. Others have been taught to communicate in sign language. The apes have learned to express their own ideas and feelings as well as just copying the signs.

Chimpanzee using a stone as a weapon

Koko, a captive gorilla in the United States, knew enough sign language to tell her keepers that she wanted a kitten for a pet.

◁ **Chimpanzee collecting water**

Map of Africa showing where gorillas and chimpanzees live

- ■ pygmy chimpanzee
- □ mountain gorilla
- ■ lowland gorilla
- ■ chimpanzee

Zaire

Uganda

Rwanda

Gabon

Congo

In Africa alone 8 square miles of forest are cleared each day. That is about the same area as an average-sized town.

Gorillas at risk

Because they are so large as well as intelligent, gorillas have little to fear from any other animal. Chimpanzees are sometimes hunted by large cats or hyenas, but the gorillas' only enemies are human. Gorillas are chiefly threatened by the destruction of the forests in which they live. They are slow to breed. Any disturbance in their quiet life means that fewer babies survive and the gorilla population gets smaller. There are fewer than 1,300 gorillas left in the world.

The gorillas that live in the mountains of East Africa are losing their forest homes at an alarming rate. There are probably only 400 of them left. They have retreated higher up the mountains where there is less food for them.

The thick coats of mountain gorillas keep out the cold ▷

Beyond the forest

Some chimpanzees have spread to more open habitats. These groups live in wooded grassland called the savannah. They have to move over much greater areas to find enough to eat.

These chimpanzees hunt together and kill animals for their food. They are better at waving sticks and throwing stones than chimpanzees in forests. They act better as a group to prevent attacks by lions, cheetahs and hyenas. Savannah chimpanzees have to stand upright to see over the tall grass.

The development of these chimpanzees has given scientists more clues about what happened to another group of primates – humans – when they first moved out of the forests.

Chimpanzees are more adaptable than gorillas. Their numbers are not declining nearly as rapidly.

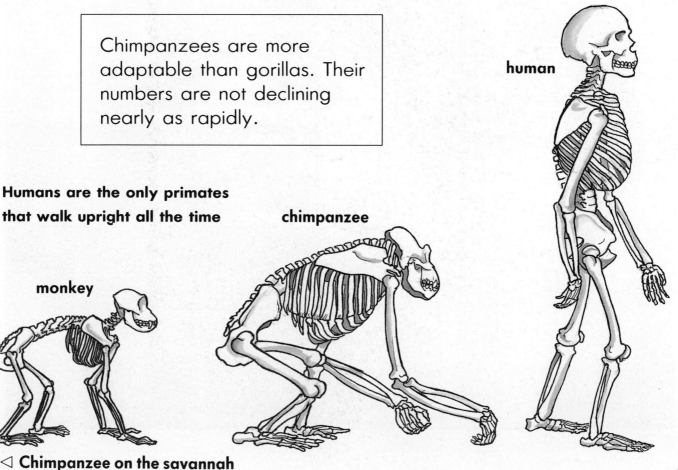

Humans are the only primates that walk upright all the time

human

chimpanzee

monkey

◁ **Chimpanzee on the savannah**

Survival file

Gorillas and chimpanzees face many dangers. The African forests they live in are disappearing fast. Local people kill them for food and also as pests. They are protected by law but poachers still kill them and sell their skulls, hands and feet to tourists. They are trapped for zoos and medical research. Some baby chimpanzees are smuggled into the Canary Islands and Spain to be used by beach photographers. The mothers are killed and many of the babies die on the way.

Chimpanzee behind bars

Protecting gorillas and chimpanzees

Scientists study gorillas and chimpanzees in Africa to learn how they live. They want to find out how apes make friends and communicate with each other. They need to know how they move around, how much space they need, what and when they eat.

Some chimpanzees are now protected in National Parks. The scientists working with chimpanzees have helped to set up these reserves. In West Africa they have tried to take captive chimpanzees back to the forests from zoos and pet owners, though this has not been easy.

Studying chimpanzees

Learning about grooming

The governments of Rwanda, Zaire and Uganda have protected the Virunga Volcanoes, almost the last home of the mountain gorilla. They have already set up anti-poaching patrols. They are trying to teach the local people and tourists more about the importance of gorillas. Now other African countries are following their example, so there is some hope the gorillas will survive.

Identification chart

This chart shows you the difference between the two kinds of chimpanzee and a gorilla. They are drawn to the same scale to show their comparative sizes.

pygmy chimpanzee

chimpanzee

Make a chimpanzee mask

1. Using a pencil and a ruler divide your card into 1-inch squares.
2. Copy one of the chimpanzee faces from the opposite page, using the squares to help you.
3. Erase the pencil squares from the face.
4. Color in the face.
5. Cut out the mask, make holes, and attach strings or elastic.
6. Now you can wear your chimpanzee mask.

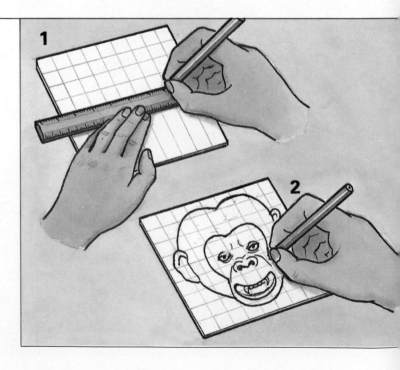

gorilla

angry

excited

playful

alert

3

4

5

6

69

The little square shows you the size of the animal. Each side represents 10 feet.

The picture opposite shows a young male Indian tiger

Chapter 3
LIONS
AND
TIGERS

Lionel Bender

Facts to Know

There are 35 different species of cats. The lion and the tiger are the biggest. All cats are hunters and meat-eaters. Lions live mainly in Africa, where they are found in open grassland and sometimes in desert and bush country. Tigers live in India and parts of China, the Soviet Union and the Far East. They prefer forest country. However, in the north of their range tigers live in snow-covered pine forests, and in the south they live in hot jungles.

Like other mammals, lions and tigers are intelligent and care for their young. But they are also very fierce animals and behave quite differently from their close relative, the domestic cat.

◁ **A male lion with its wildebeest prey**

Big cats

Lions and tigers are both 'big cats'. This is a group of the cat family that also includes the Leopard, Snow Leopard and the Jaguar. A domestic cat measures about 70 cm (28 in) from nose to tip of tail and weighs around 4 kg (9 lb). A lion can measure up to 3 m (10 ft) in length and weigh up to 240 kg (520 lb). A tiger can grow to 3.6 m (12 ft) and 350 kg (770 lb). Male lions and tigers grow 25 per cent bigger than females.

Like all cats, lions and tigers have strong muscles for running and jumping, and sharp teeth and claws for gripping and tearing their prey. But big cats have particularly large heads. They also roar rather than yowl and purr only as they breathe out.

Sabre-toothed tigers lived 25 to 2 million years ago. They used their huge front upper teeth, or fangs, to pierce the necks of their victims. They had fangs 20 cm (8 in) long and used to kill elephants.

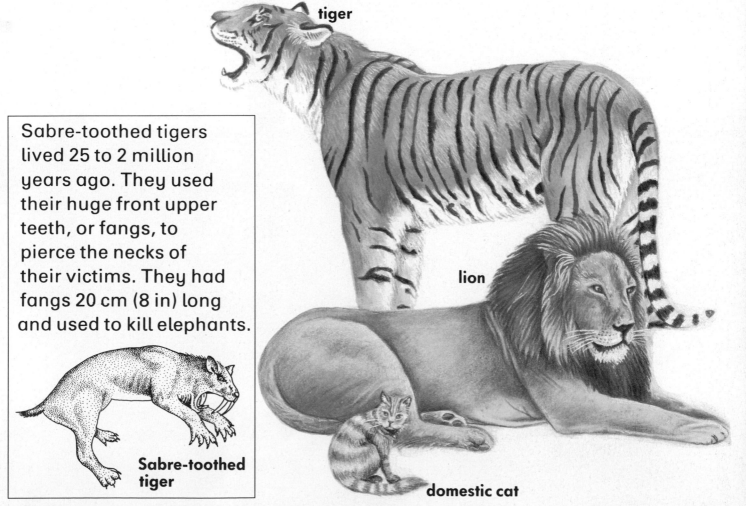

Sabre-toothed tiger

tiger

lion

domestic cat

◁ **The tiger's stripes help it blend into its forest home**

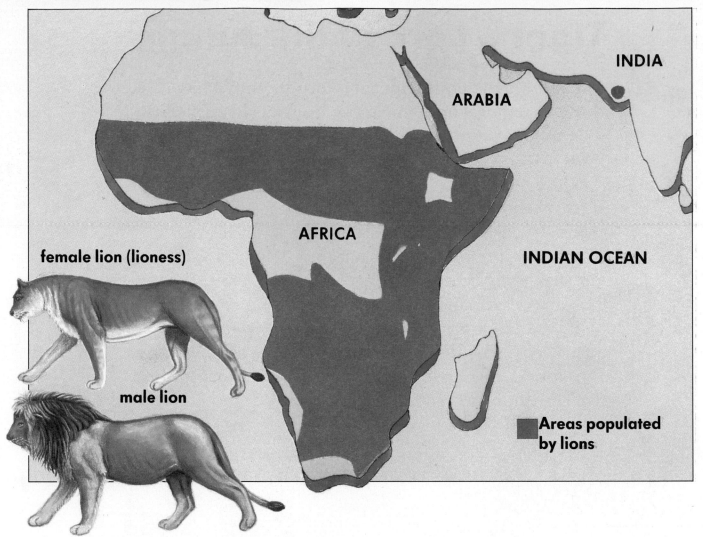

female lion (lioness)

male lion

INDIA

ARABIA

AFRICA

INDIAN OCEAN

■ Areas populated by lions

Lion – King of Beasts

The lion is often called the King of Beasts. An adult male lion is larger than most meat-eaters and is much larger than any person. It has a long, stately mane of thick fur around its neck and its often calm nature adds to its majestic appearance.

The lion is the only cat that lives in groups. Sometimes a male lion may travel alone or in a small group with other males. But lions love company. They live together in prides. These are usually made up of a few adult males, ten or more adult female lions and their young. The males defend the pride's feeding and resting areas. They also prevent male lions of other prides from mating with their females.

77

Tiger – Lord of the Jungle

The tiger is the lion's closest relative. Only a few thousand years ago, these two animals lived side by side across central southern Asia and India. Today the tiger is most common in northern India.

Tigers vary in size and color from place to place. The biggest tiger, the Siberian, can reach 13 feet in length. It has a yellowish coat that is tinged with red in the summer. The coat is also very thick, which keeps the animal warm in the cold winters. The smallest tiger, the Sumatran, grows to about 8 feet long. It has a reddish-yellow coat with thin, closely set stripes. The tiger's coat helps it blend in with the foliage and dry grass of its home.

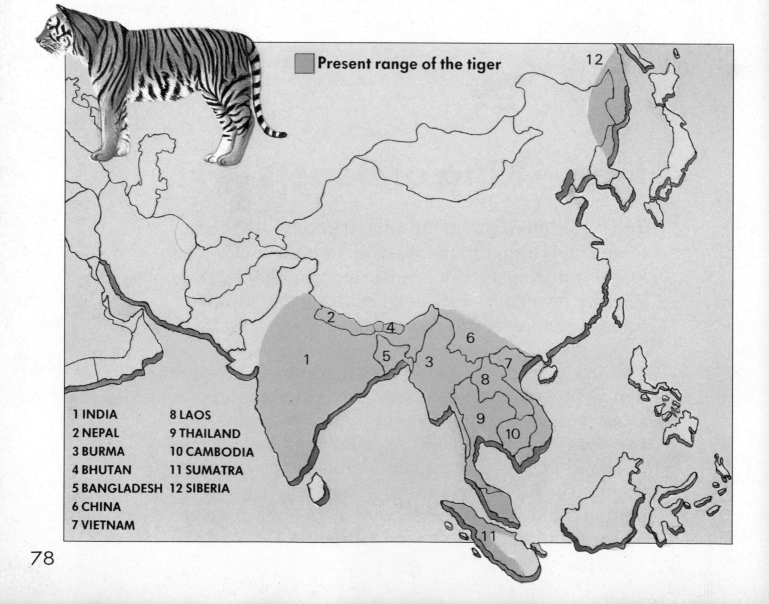

Present range of the tiger

1 INDIA
2 NEPAL
3 BURMA
4 BHUTAN
5 BANGLADESH
6 CHINA
7 VIETNAM
8 LAOS
9 THAILAND
10 CAMBODIA
11 SUMATRA
12 SIBERIA

Teeth and claws

Lions and tigers are expert hunters. They use their teeth and claws as killing weapons. Their jaws are short and powerful, which gives them great biting strength. Cats have 30 teeth. The biggest are the upper canines, the fangs, which are used for grabbing and piercing. The incisors, the front teeth, are small but sharp. They are used for making a nip in the skin of prey. The side or cheek teeth are used like scissors to slice off lumps of meat to swallow.

Like all cats, lions and tigers have soft pads of skin on their paws so they can creep up silently on their prey. The paws have claws for gripping and tearing flesh. The animals scratch at trees to sharpen their claws.

Lions and tigers can pull back their claws inside sheaths, folds of skin, between their toes. The claws are extended only when the animals pounce to kill.

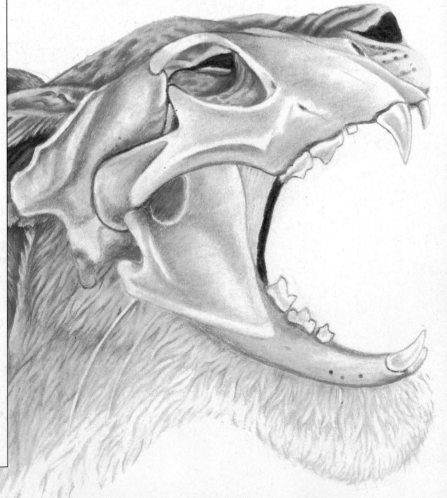

Head of a lioness, showing strong skull and teeth

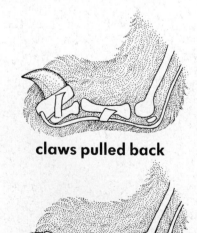

claws pulled back

claws extended

80

Catching prey

Lions that live in open grassland, where there is little cover to hide in, often hunt at night and in groups. Lions that live among tangled bush often hunt by day, and then alone or in pairs. Usually the adult lionesses do the hunting. They are lighter in weight than the males and therefore more agile and faster moving. Also, without a mane, they are less easily seen and can wrestle better in close combat. Often several lionesses hunt together. They spread out and surround the prey. Then, when they are about 100 feet from the prey, they attack.

Tigers hunt alone and at night. Sometimes a tiger waits for its prey near a water hole. Then it creeps up on the animal. With a quick dash, it rushes at its victim, knocks it to the ground, and grabs the animal's neck with its mighty jaws.

Big cats kill their prey by biting and squeezing the victim's throat. This means the animal cannot breathe, and so it dies quickly without a struggle.

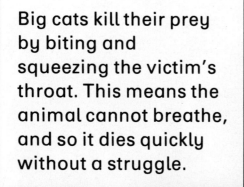

A lioness attacking a wildebeest

Food and feeding

An adult lion or tiger needs about 33 pounds of meat a day. A lion hunts only when it must eat and takes one animal at a time. It kills one or two large animals each week. A tiger will kill several animals if it can, but feeds on only one or two of them. Many of the kills are eaten by wild dogs and other tigers.

All members of a lion's pride share a kill. The prey is eaten on the spot or is dragged to a place where it can be guarded. The adult males eat first, then the females and young. A tiger pulls its victim into cover before feeding. When it has eaten enough, it hides the kill by putting grass or earth over it. It returns to the carcass for several days to feed.

The lioness kills prey and drags it to the pride.

The male lions eat first . . .

Lions eat mainly wildebeest, gazelle, waterbuck and zebra. Tigers eat deer, wild pigs and water buffalo. Where they live near farms they also eat sheep and goats.

. . . then the lionesses and cubs eat.

84

Family life

Within a pride of lions, the adult females are usually sisters, cousins or mothers and daughters. Each may have several young. The adult males are often brothers, but are not close relatives of the other pride members. Male lions are driven out of a pride when they are about three years old. They often live alone for a year or two, then compete with other adult males to take over a pride and become its leaders or defenders.

A typical tiger family consists of a mother tiger and her one or two young. The young leave the family when they are about two and a half years old. Adult male tigers mostly live alone. They share the company of female tigers only at mating time.

Young adult male lions that have just taken over a pride may kill cubs already in the pride. They then mate with the females. This means only their own young grow to be adults.

2. Mother of lioness (1)

1. Lioness

5. Son of lioness (1)

4. Daughter of lioness (3)

A tigress with her cubs

3. Daughter of lioness (1)

6. Outsider (male)

**7. Half-brother males
(not related to females)**

8. Son of lioness (3)

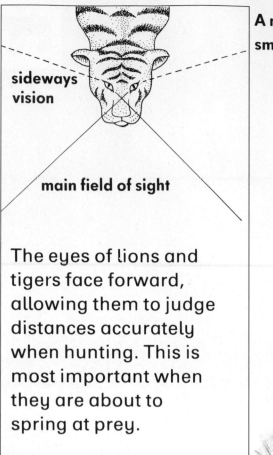

sideways vision

main field of sight

The eyes of lions and tigers face forward, allowing them to judge distances accurately when hunting. This is most important when they are about to spring at prey.

A male tiger wrinkles its lips on smelling a female that is ready to mate.

Senses and scents

In daylight, lions and tigers can see about as well as we can. But at night, when they usually hunt, their sight is six times better than ours. Their ear flaps are large and can move around to collect sounds from most directions. The whiskers around their mouths are long, stiff and very sensitive to touch. They are especially useful for finding a way through grass at night without making a sound.

These big cats use their senses of smell and taste mostly for sniffing and tasting the scents of one another. Males will sniff out females at mating time and all adults use body scents and urine to mark out their territories.

A lion sprays a bush to mark its territory ▷

Territories

A tiger sometimes travels 6 miles in a single
night in search of food and water. In a year it may
move over an area of 58 square miles, which is
known as the animal's territory. Occasionally, the
tiger meets other tigers whose territories cross its own.
Each animal then marks the edge of its territory. It uses
its strong-smelling urine and dung and also rubs
scent from glands under its chin on twigs and branches.

Lion prides also have territories. Where food is easy to
find, territories may measure only 8 square
miles. When prides meet, the adults may roar loudly
at one another. Adult males from each pride also fight
with each other to defend their home areas.

Male lions fight to defend their territories

Two Indian tigers lash out at each other with their paws ▷

Courtship

Male and female lions are able to breed when they are about three to four years old. Pregnancy lasts for about 16 weeks in both lions and tigers. Lions may mate at any time of the year. However, female tigers mate only when their cubs can be born at a time when there is plenty of prey.

The female is willing to mate on only two or three days during each breeding season. At this time the males often fight with one another for the chance to mate with a female. The winner then approaches the female. At first the two animals growl and snarl, but then they rub heads and lick each other before mating. Males often mate with many females.

A male lion grabs a female's neck during courtship

92

Male and female tigers rub heads before mating ▷

Growing up

A pregnant lioness or tigress usually gives birth to two or three cubs. At birth, the cubs measure about 24 inches from head to tip of tail and weigh 2-4 pounds. The mother leaves the cubs in a hiding place each time she hunts. But often the cubs are found and killed by hyenas and other predators.

The cubs feed on their mother's milk until they are about three months old. Then they start to eat meat. They are not strong enough to fend for themselves until they are about two. Their mother then has her next litter of cubs and loses interest in her first offspring. The young adults begin their independent lives. Lions and tigers live for about 15 to 20 years.

Young Sumatran tiger cubs

Lion cubs feeding on their mother's milk ▷

Survival file

Lions and tigers have suffered greatly from human activity. Many thousands have been killed over the past hundred years, either for sport or to provide fur coats or rugs. Occasionally, when a lion or tiger is desperate for food, it will kill farm animals or even people. This can be a reason to destroy the animal. But many of these beatiful animals are trapped or poisoned simply because they *might* be dangerous. There are strict laws about hunting lions and tigers, but poaching and illegal trading still go on.

Tiger skins are still sold in shops in some countries

Today, the greatest threat to these big cats is the spread of villages and farms into their natural homes. In parts of Africa and India, places have been set aside as reserves for lions and tigers. There they can roam and hunt freely. In some reserves, populations of lions and tigers have increased. But throughout Africa, the long-term survival of lions is doubtful. And the most common type of tiger, the Indian, numbers no more than about 3,500. Eighty years ago there were 40,000.

This electrified wooden man scares off tigers

Lions and tigers breed in Safari Parks

Another threat to the survival of lions and tigers is the reduction in the amount of food they have available. Zebras, gazelles, buffaloes, wildebeest and deer are the major prey of big cats. These animals are killed in large numbers by people, either for food or to protect crops.

However, in zoos and wildlife parks around the world, lions and tigers are being bred successfully. Scientists no longer need to take animals from the wild to study them. And we do not have to trample over their homelands to see them.

Identification chart

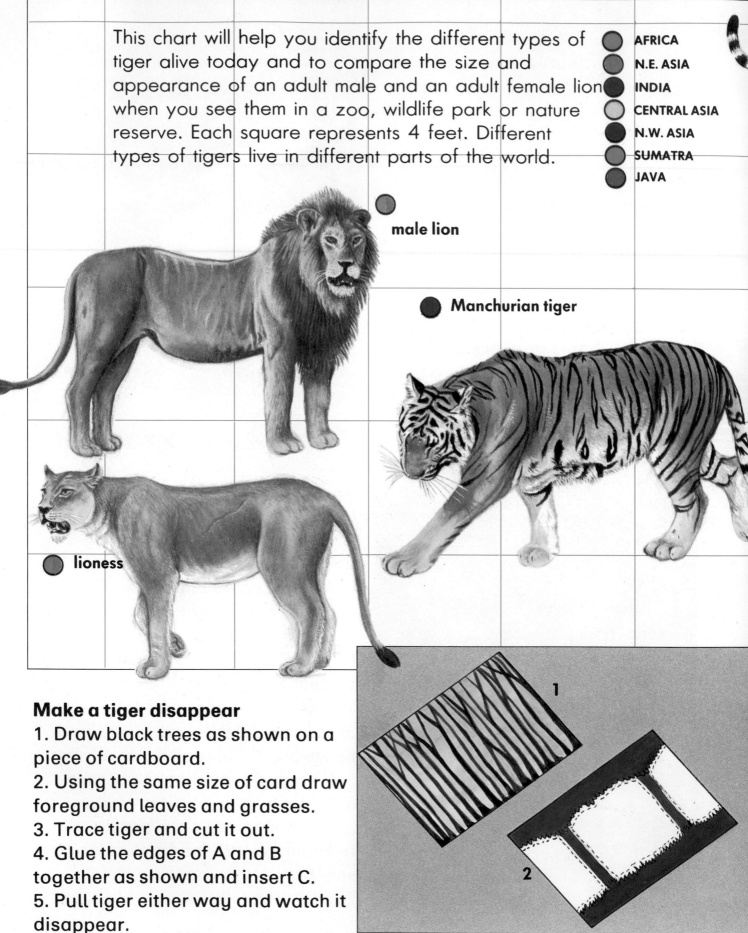

This chart will help you identify the different types of tiger alive today and to compare the size and appearance of an adult male and an adult female lion when you see them in a zoo, wildlife park or nature reserve. Each square represents 4 feet. Different types of tigers live in different parts of the world.

AFRICA
N.E. ASIA
INDIA
CENTRAL ASIA
N.W. ASIA
SUMATRA
JAVA

male lion

Manchurian tiger

lioness

1

2

Make a tiger disappear

1. Draw black trees as shown on a piece of cardboard.
2. Using the same size of card draw foreground leaves and grasses.
3. Trace tiger and cut it out.
4. Glue the edges of A and B together as shown and insert C.
5. Pull tiger either way and watch it disappear.

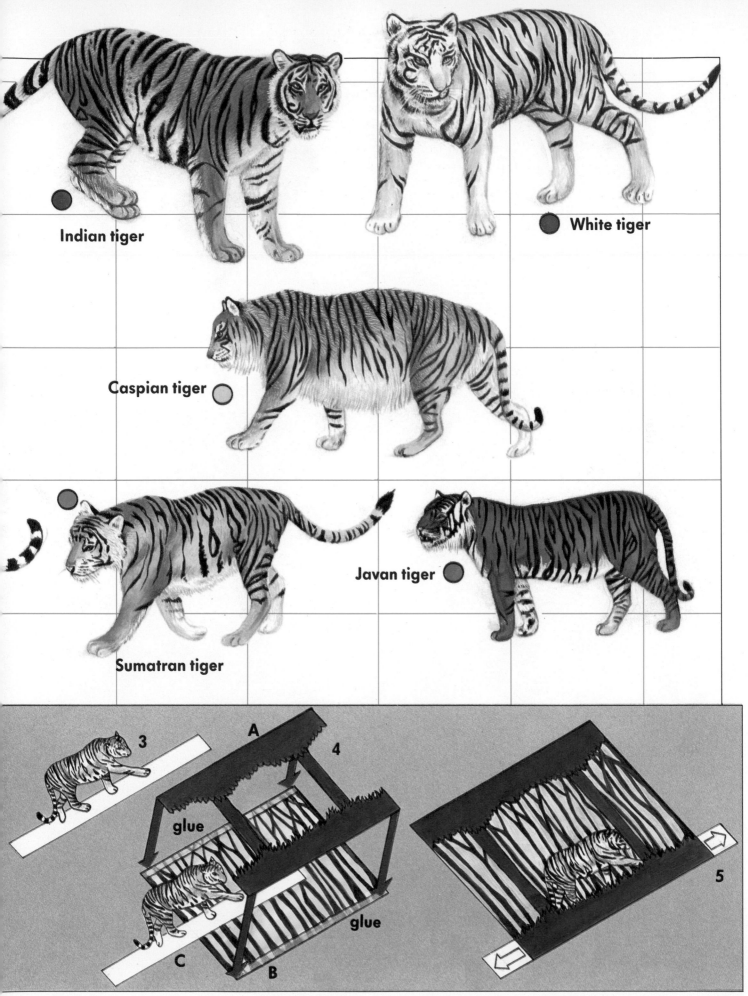

Indian tiger

White tiger

Caspian tiger

Sumatran tiger

Javan tiger

3

A

4

glue

glue

C

B

5

The little square shows
you the size of the
insect. Each side
represents 2 inches.

The picture opposite shows a Gum Moth Caterpillar

Chapter 4
POISONOUS INSECTS

Lionel Bender

Facts to Know

Insects are one of the most successful groups of animals. There are over a million different species and they live in all parts of the world. Insects owe their success to several features. Most species have wings and can fly. They can move freely to find food or mates, or to escape their enemies. They have a hard waterproof outer covering, the exoskeleton. This provides protection and allows them to live in dry areas. They can also reproduce in great numbers.

Many insects are also equipped with weapons, both to frighten off attackers and to kill the animals on which they feed. Some produce poisons. Others sting their attackers or have nasty spines that can cause swelling and blistering of the skin.

◁ **The bright colors of Harlequin Bugs warn birds not to eat them**

Some insects pierce victim's skin with needle-like mouthparts. They inject a deadly poison from glands in the head.

A Digger Wasp (*Astata boops*)

mouthparts

victim

sting

mouthparts

Insect weapons

All insects have specialized mouthparts. The Tsetse Fly feeds on the blood of mammals, including humans. It has piercing and sucking mouthparts. As the fly feeds, it injects saliva into the wound. The saliva contains tiny animals that produce harmful chemicals inside the victim's body. Assassin bugs have mouthparts with glands that produce a poison as the insects feed. The poison kills or stuns the victim.

At the rear of most insects' bodies is an egg or sperm tube. In female bees, wasps and ants, the tube has become a pointed sting that injects poison. Some insects possess poisonous chemicals inside their bodies.

**Bombardier beetle
(*Brachinus*)**

Bombardier and oil beetles

Bombardier beetles frighten off would-be attackers, such as ants, toads and mice, by spraying them with boiling hot liquids. The liquids cause the attacker's skin to swell up and become painful. The spray is shot out of the rear of the beetle's body through a fine nozzle. Some non-flying ground beetles squirt out acids when disturbed. These chemicals burn the skin and cause serious damage to the eyes of mammals.

Oil beetles store a poisonous chemical in their bodies. The larvae of some African leaf beetles are so poisonous that native people in the Kalahari Desert use them to tip their arrows when they hunt birds and large mammals.

◁ **The black and yellow markings of this Palm Beetle warn off predators**

Leaf and bark beetles

Each year, leaf-feeding beetles cause millions of dollars worth of damage to crops. They spread diseases from plant to plant so that seeds do not form. The beetles carry microscopic creatures—mostly bacteria (germs)—inside their bodies. The bacteria get into the plants as the insects feed. They produce poisons that prevent plants from growing properly.

Female bark beetles bore into the wood of trees to lay their eggs. These beetles carry a tiny fungus that causes a deadly disease in the trees. When the beetle larvae hatch, they chew out tunnels in the wood. At the same time the fungus clogs up the tubes which carry the tree's sap. The tree dies within only a few weeks.

Oak Bark Beetle (*Scolytus vitricatus*)

Dutch elm disease is caused by a fungus carried by the Elm Bark Beetle. The larvae tunnel through the wood. When adult, they bore through the bark of the tree and fly off.

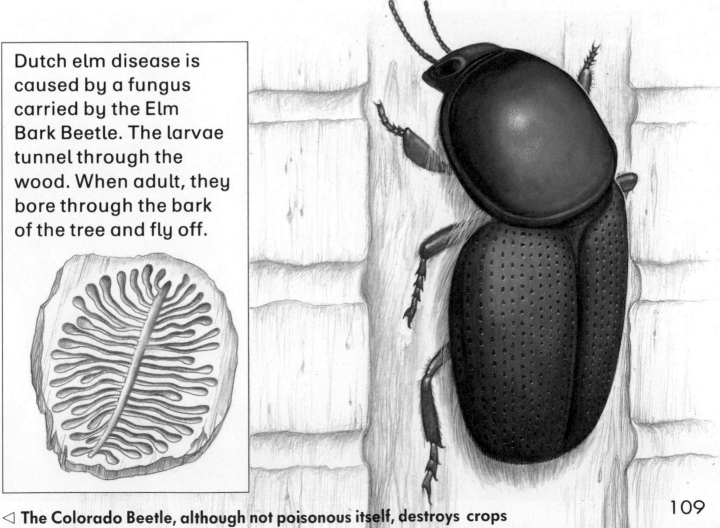

◁ **The Colorado Beetle, although not poisonous itself, destroys crops**

Termites and leaf insects

Termites are probably best known for the giant mounds of earth they build. The mounds house their colonies of millions of eggs, larvae and adults. But snouted termites are also well-known for the sticky and irritating chemicals they produce to defend themselves against ants, their arch enemies. The soldier termites squirt the chemicals from their snouts.

Leaf and stick insects are shaped and colored to blend in with their surroundings. Usually they go unnoticed by animals that eat insects. But if they are disturbed, some of them squirt their attackers with digested food. This contains acids that burn their victims' skin and eyes.

A leaf insect is poised to squirt irritating chemicals

Soldier Snouted Termites protect two fellow worker termites ▷

Fleas spread diseases because they reproduce in great numbers and they can move easily from victim to victim. The Human Flea can travel 12 inches with each leap.

Fleas and lice

Fleas and lice survive by feeding on other living creatures. Some attack people, pets and farm animals to suck their blood. The Human Body Louse has mouthparts that include a needle-like hollow tube. This can pierce a person's skin, and the blood is sucked through it. The insect's jab causes irritation. As the person scratches his or her skin, a germ that may be carried by the louse gets into the body. This causes an unpleasant disease called typhus.

In the 14th and 16th centuries, the Rat Flea was responsible for the deaths of millions of people throughout Europe. The flea can carry a germ from rats to people. This germ produces a poison causing a disease known as bubonic plague, or the Black Death.

A Human Flea jumping

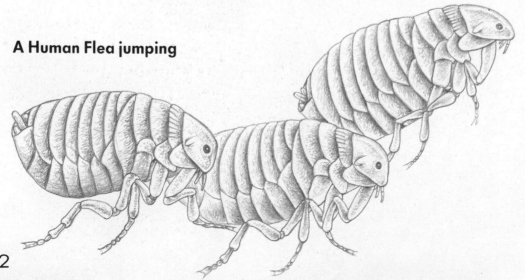

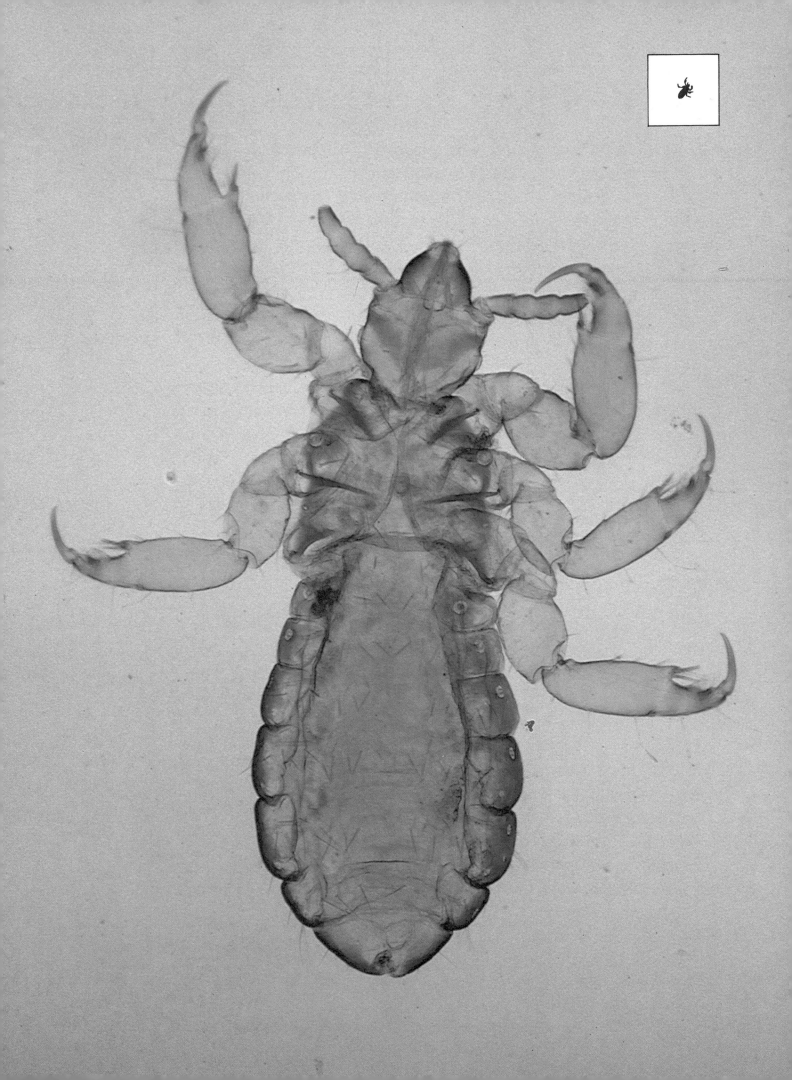

Bugs

Bugs are insects with piercing and sucking mouthparts, which are housed in a long beak-like structure. Assassin bugs hunt and feed on other insects. A few produce scents to attract bees. They seize the bees with their forelegs and inject a poisonous saliva into them. They can also squirt the saliva at attackers. Other assassin bugs are called kissing bugs because they often bite people in the face and inject a poison that has been known to kill.

Shield bugs feed on plants. They are often brightly colored and have strange shapes. This warns other animals that they have poisonous chemicals in their bodies and are not to be eaten.

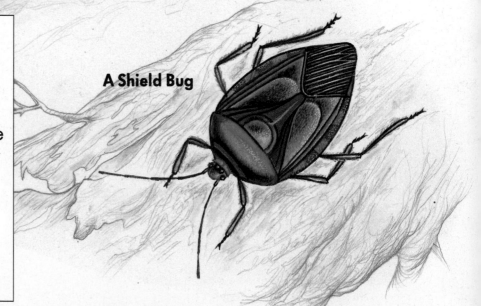

An assassin bug poisoning a fly

A Shield Bug

The assassin bug *Rhodnius* can carry tiny animals that cause a deadly disease in people. These animals pass out of the bug in its feces as it feeds on a person's blood. They form poisons that attack the liver and heart.

An assassin bug sinks its needle-like mouthparts into a Shield Bug ▷

A female *Anopheles* mosquito in the act of taking a blood meal from a human

Malaria is caused by tiny animals carried by the female *Anopheles* mosquito. The animals are injected into a person as an infected mosquito feeds. They produce a poison which causes fever.

Flies

True flies have one pair of wings. They also have sucking mouthparts and feed on liquid foods of all kinds, from nectar to blood. They do not produce poisons themselves, but they carry germs that can cause illness and damage in other living creatures. The Malaria Mosquito causes the death of at least one million people every year in Africa and Asia. Tsetse Flies can cause a disease called sleeping sickness.

Bluebottles and houseflies love to eat rotting meat and fresh animal droppings. As they do so, they pick up germs on their mouthparts and feet. When the insects land on food in our homes, they leave the germs behind. If we eat the food, the germs can cause stomach upsets.

A Tsetse Fly rests on the surface of a person's skin and injects its saliva ▷

Butterflies and moths

Adult butterflies and moths can fly away from danger. But the caterpillars are easy prey. To protect themselves, many caterpillars have weapons. Others collect poisons from the plants they eat and store them inside their bodies. In some species, the poisons remain in the adults.

The Puss Moth Caterpillar warns off its enemies by showing its "face" markings when disturbed. It can also squirt an acid at an attacker. Slug caterpillars have tufts of sharp stinging hairs coated with poisons which can cause pain and swelling. Caterpillars of the South American Emperor Moth can inject a poison which causes serious bleeding.

The poisonous rear of the larva of the Death's Head Hawk Moth warns off predators

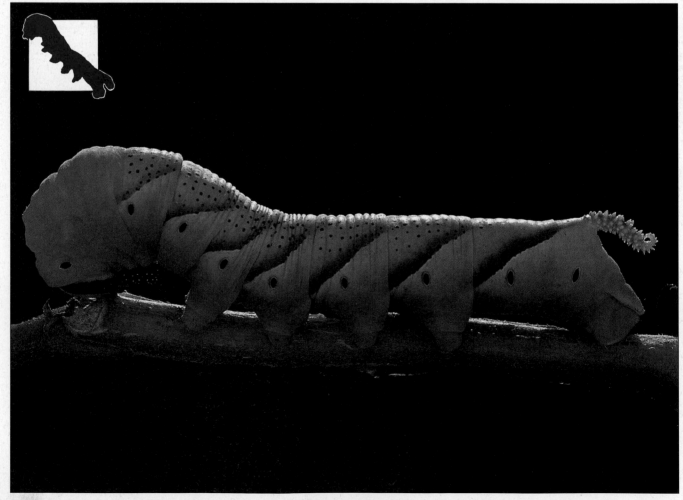

The Monarch Butterfly takes up chemicals from plants and makes itself poisonous to eat ▷

Ants and sawflies

Soldier ants guard an ant colony's nest. Most soldier ants have mouthparts and poisons that can be used to fight off attackers. A nip from the jaws of a soldier Black Bulldog Ant can kill an adult human within 15 minutes. Among Wood Ants and Army Ants, the soldiers can spray acids as a means of defense. One of these acids is called formic acid. It causes a painful burning sensation if sprayed into the eyes.

Sawfly larvae look like caterpillars. Those of the Australian Sawfly *Perga* feed only on the leaves of eucalyptus trees. They collect a foul-smelling chemical from the leaves. If the larvae are disturbed, they squirt the chemical from their mouths.

Sawfly larvae wave their poisonous bodies in a threat display

A Wood Ant produces a droplet of acid from its rear ▷

Hunting wasps

Wasps will sting people if threatened, but they are also useful insects. Many hunt and kill insect pests, such as caterpillars. Hunting wasps live alone and not in large swarms — they are not social insects. The females use their stings to capture other insects and spiders in order to feed their larvae.

A female Thread-waisted Wasp builds a nest in loose earth. Then she hunts for a caterpillar and paralyzes it with her sting. She drags the live caterpillar back to her nest using her legs. She lays an egg on her victim and closes up the nest entrance with small stones. When the wasp larva hatches, it feeds on the paralyzed caterpillar.

Velvet Ants are actually wasps. The females look like ants because they do not have wings. They hunt and paralyze bees and other wasps to feed to their larvae. Some attack Tsetse Flies and so could be useful to prevent sleeping sickness.

American Thread-waisted Wasp putting prey into its nest

◁ **A hunting wasp has successfully poisoned a tarantula**

Bees

Bees are also useful insects – they carry pollen from flower to flower to make fruits grow. But a bee's sting can sometimes be deadly. One person attacked by wild bees was stung 2,243 times and recovered. Recently in South and Central America, however, a type of bee has developed that has killed more than 150 people, each time with just a single sting.

The Honeybee has a poisonous sting that it uses only in self-defense. The poison causes swelling and pain. The sting has tiny hooks that prevent the bee from pulling it out of its attacker. Soon after the bee uses its sting it dies. Bumblebees do not have a hooked sting and can use their sting many times.

Stinging Mason Bees build a nest of mud

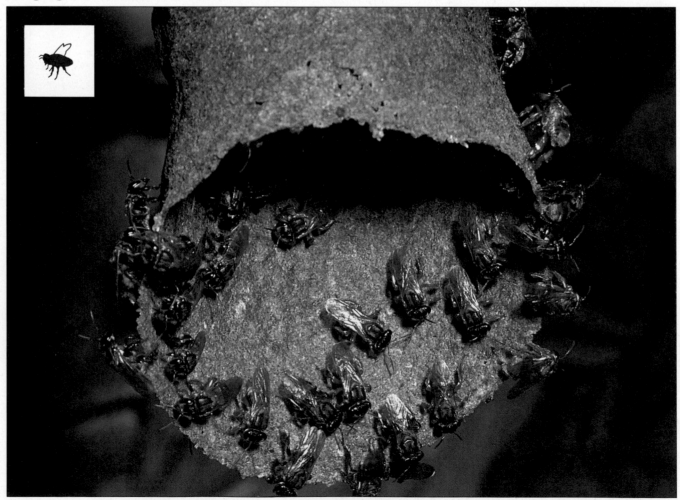

Worker bees use their stings to defend themselves and the hive's queen ▷

Survival file

Poisonous insects such as the Malaria Mosquito and Elm Bark Beetle are pests. They are harmful to plants and animals. People often try to kill such insects by spraying them with chemicals called insecticides. But these chemicals kill all insects. Some insects are extremely helpful. Honeybees pollinate flowers, produce honey that we eat, and create waxes that we use to make candles and polishes. Ants and termites help in the breakdown of dead animal and plant material, which helps to make the soil rich and fertile.

A beekeeper wears protective clothing to prevent being stung

Because insecticides affect all insects, scientists are looking at other ways of killing insect pests. One way is to actually use poisonous insects. In some tree plantations, ladybirds have been introduced to get rid of aphids and scales. These are insects that feed on leaves, fruits and soft stems and so weaken the trees.

In parts of the United States, the Seven-spot Ladybird is used to control aphids that destroy potato plants by sucking up the plants' juices. Also in the United States the larvae of houseflies, which as adults contaminate fresh food, are used to control bark beetles and weevils that feed on crops.

Ladybirds feed on aphids

This hunting wasp injects its larvae into the larvae of wasps that feed on trees

Probably the most useful insects for pest control are the hunting wasps. More than 180 different species are being used around the world today to control the numbers of harmful and nuisance insects. Many species of hunting wasp prey on only one or two specific insects, such as certain caterpillars. So farmers can introduce a particular species of hunting wasp to kill a pest that is damaging a crop.

Identification chart

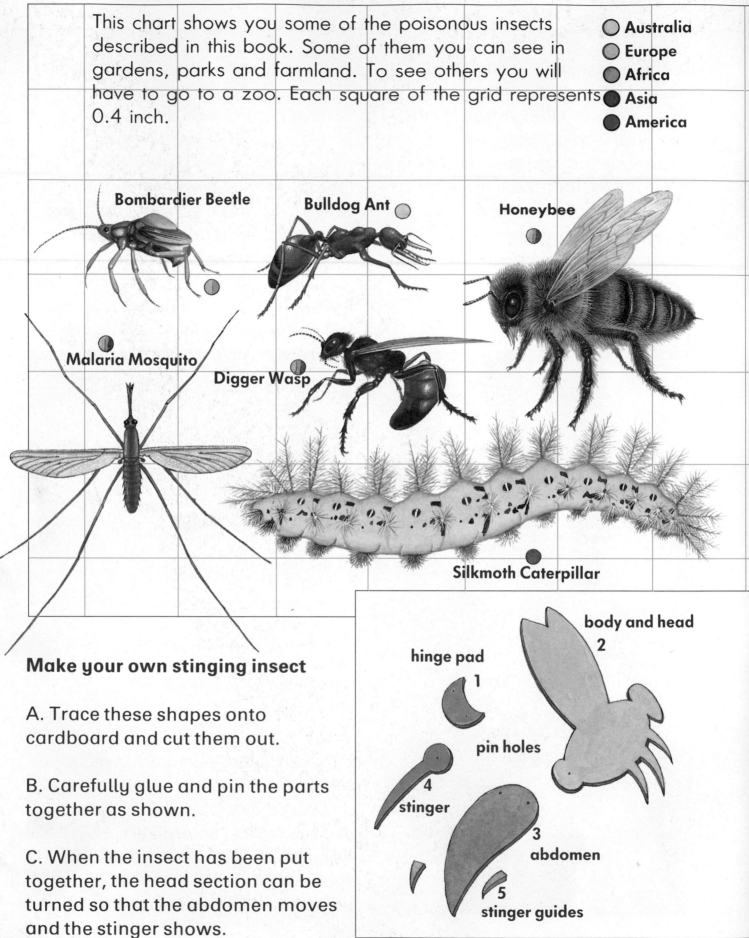

This chart shows you some of the poisonous insects described in this book. Some of them you can see in gardens, parks and farmland. To see others you will have to go to a zoo. Each square of the grid represents 0.4 inch.

- Australia
- Europe
- Africa
- Asia
- America

Bombardier Beetle

Bulldog Ant

Honeybee

Malaria Mosquito

Digger Wasp

Silkmoth Caterpillar

Make your own stinging insect

A. Trace these shapes onto cardboard and cut them out.

B. Carefully glue and pin the parts together as shown.

C. When the insect has been put together, the head section can be turned so that the abdomen moves and the stinger shows.

hinge pad
1

body and head
2

pin holes

4
stinger

3
abdomen

5
stinger guides

128

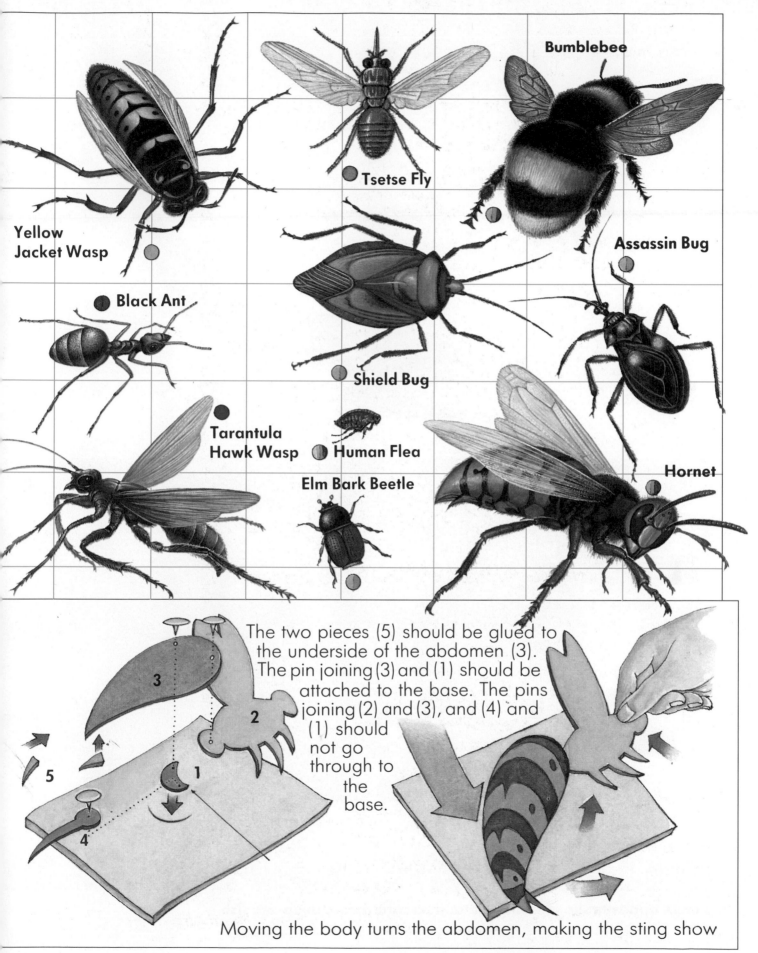

Bumblebee

Tsetse Fly

Yellow Jacket Wasp

Assassin Bug

Black Ant

Shield Bug

Tarantula Hawk Wasp

Human Flea

Elm Bark Beetle

Hornet

The two pieces (5) should be glued to the underside of the abdomen (3). The pin joining (3) and (1) should be attached to the base. The pins joining (2) and (3), and (4) and (1) should not go through to the base.

Moving the body turns the abdomen, making the sting show

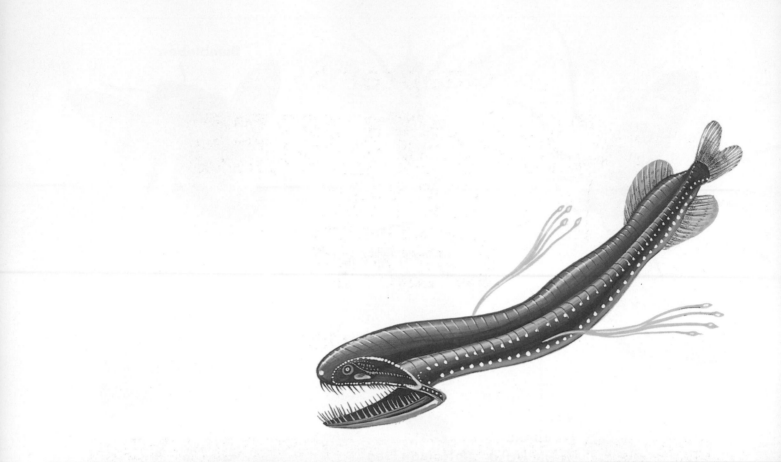

The little square shows
you how big the animal is compared
to a person. Each side represents
.75 feet.

The picture opposite shows a snaggletooth, a carnivorous deep-sea fish

Chapter 5
CREATURES OF THE DEEP

Lionel Bender

Facts to Know

Two-thirds of the Earth's surface is covered by water.
Most of this water is in seas and oceans, which are very
deep in places. Some underwater trenches reach
4.2 miles below sea level. In the open seas, sunlight
only penetrates the top 650 feet of water. As plants
need sunlight, they cannot grow any deeper. Below this
"light zone," it gets increasingly dark and there is less
food for animals to eat. Beyond 6,000 feet there is
hardly a glimmer of light. At these depths the pressure of
the water is immense—a person would be crushed
instantly.

Many animals that live in deep water have bizarre
shapes, structures and behaviors. This is because they
must be adapted to survive in darkness, without live
plant food and under great pressure.

◁ **The fearsome head of an Angler Fish**

Ocean depths

Animals live at all depths of the oceans, though they become fewer as you descend. Differences in light, pressure and the amount of salt in the water create distinct natural zones. The upper zone contains the greatest number and variety of fish. The surface waters are also rich in invertebrates (animals without backbones) like octopuses, lobsters and jellyfish.

Marine mammals, such as whales, and reptiles, such as turtles, dive deep in the oceans. But they must return to the surface regularly to breathe. Some 2,000 species of fish, including the Angler and Lantern Fish, spend their whole lives in the depths. On the ocean floor live burrowing worms, Sea Cucumbers, sponges and shellfish.

Sea Cucumbers are found on the ocean floor

1. **Flying Fish**
2. **Octopus**
3. **Great White Shark**
4. **Sea Gooseberry**
5. **Lobster**
6. **Mackerel**
7. **Sperm Whale**
8. **Squid**
9. **Starfish**
10. **Turtle**
11. **Lantern Fish**
12. **Angler Fish**
13. **Deep-sea Shrimp**
14. **Tripod Fish**
15. **Sea Sponge**

Euphotic zone

Bathyal zone

Abyssal zone

The top zone of the ocean is the euphotic zone. This zone ends where light can no longer penetrate the water. Beneath it are the bathyal and abyssal zones. At night, some mid-water animals swim to the surface to feed. Deep-water animals rarely leave the abyssal zone.

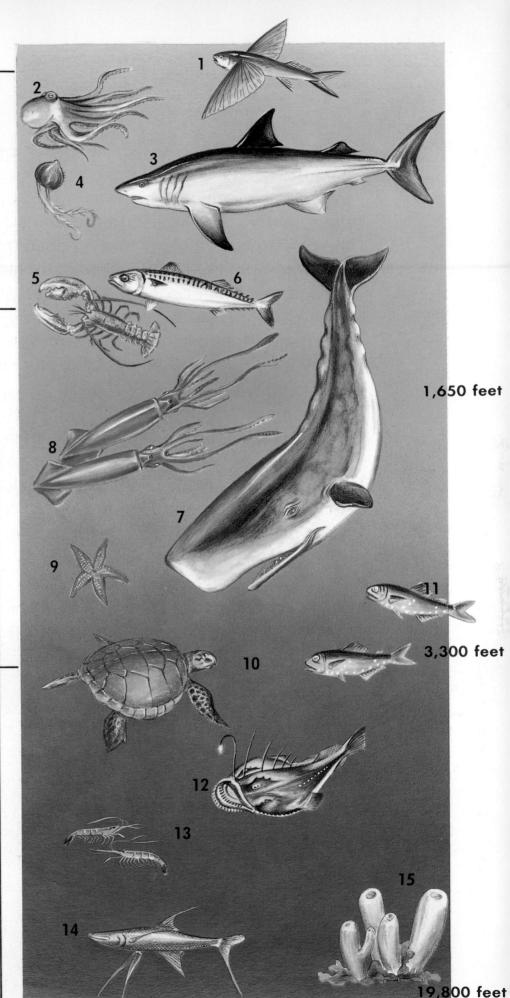

1,650 feet

3,300 feet

19,800 feet

Food chains

There are no plants living in the ocean depths. But all creatures of the deep ultimately depend on plants for their survival. Plants use the energy of sunlight to make their own food. Animals cannot do this. Instead they get their energy by eating plants, other animals, or both. Tiny free-floating plants called phytoplankton form the base of every marine food chain. Phytoplankton grow and multiply in the surface waters. They are eaten by invertebrates and fish. These are preyed upon in turn by larger fish, such as sharks, and by other predators like squid and whales.

When these plants and animals die, their remains fall to the bottom of the ocean. This "rain" of food is eaten by the scavengers of the deep, which include Sea Cucumbers, shrimps and Fan Worms. Predators – the hunters of the deep – feed on the scavengers and on each other.

Deep-sea shrimp use their claws to seize large pieces of food

The Great White Shark often hunts for smaller fish in deep water ▷

Big and small

In 1878 a Giant Squid 55 feet long was found stranded on a beach in Newfoundland. It weighed more than two tons. This species lives at depths down to 2,000 feet, where it hunts and eats fish, shellfish and other squid. It is the world's largest soft-bodied animal. But even it is dwarfed by the Sperm Whale, which can grow to 68 feet and weigh 77 tons. It mainly preys on squid. The complete body of a 39 foot Giant Squid has been found in a Sperm Whale's stomach.

Probably the most common fish in the ocean are the Bristlemouths. These live 1,650 feet or more beneath the surface, where they feed on small shellfish. Bristlemouths are tiny—each one is smaller than your thumb. Together with the equally small Hatchet and Lantern Fish, they make up 90 percent of all deep-sea predators.

Oarfish

The Oarfish has a body like a ribbon and a head shaped like that of a horse. If a person could dive deep enough, he would be tiny next to this 30-foot long fish. We believe that Oarfish feed on shellfish. Almost nothing else is known about its habits.

Two tiny deep-sea predators, a Lantern Fish (above) and a Hatchet Fish ▷

Stretching Its Tentacles

Everette Rios, an intern, squirted water on the body of a 25-foot-long squid yesterday at the American Museum of Natural History to prevent it from drying out.

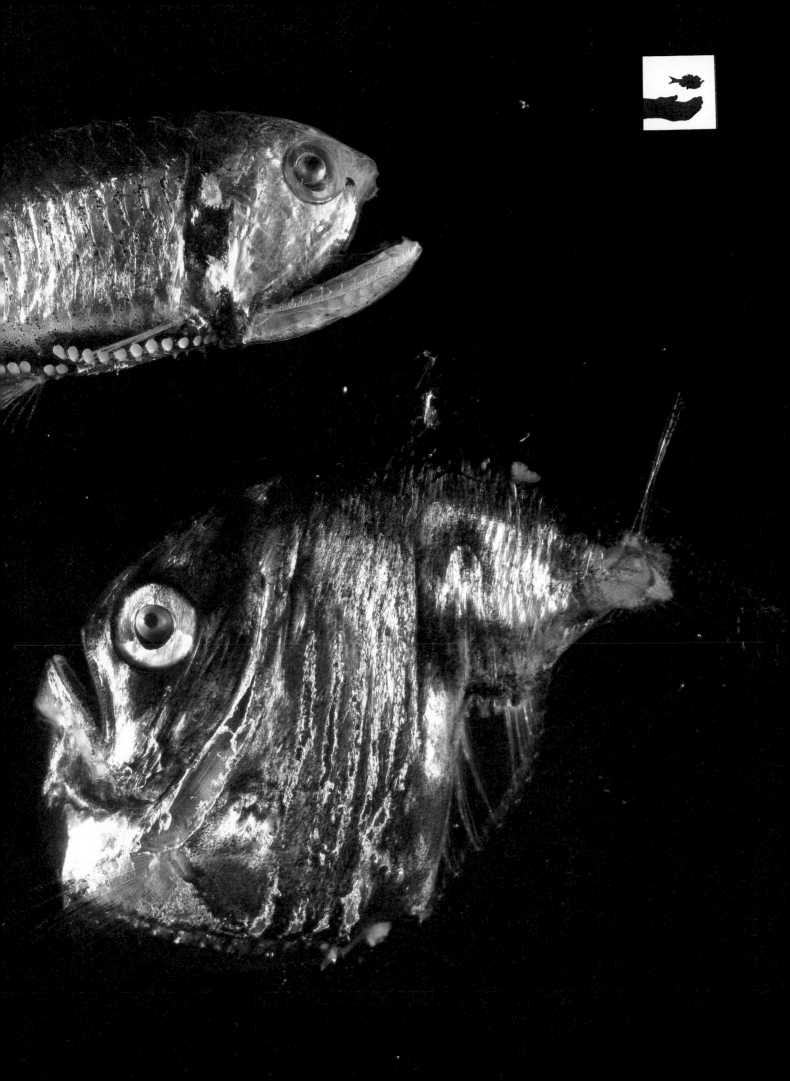

Huge jaws

Swallowers, gulpers, loosejaws, snaggletooths and dragons – these are just some of the names given to deep-sea fish. All these animals have huge gaping mouths and fearsome teeth. Because it is impossible to search for food in the darkness, they swim along with their mouths wide open, ready to gobble up anything edible that comes along. Sometimes, their victim is one of their own kind – by accident they are cannibals.

Swallowers and Viper Fish are about 6 inches long. They can gobble up prey twice their own size. Their huge jaws, lined with curved, fang-like teeth, take up most of their heads. The fish use their teeth to stab prey and pull it into their mouths. When they swallow, their heads appear to become separated from their bodies. Their stomachs can stretch enormously, as if they were made of elastic. A large meal may keep a Viper Fish going for several days.

Viper Fish

During the day Viper Fish feed in the deepest waters. At night they migrate towards the surface, where the fish they prey on are more common. It is also easier for them to escape their predators in the dark of night. These include whales and sharks.

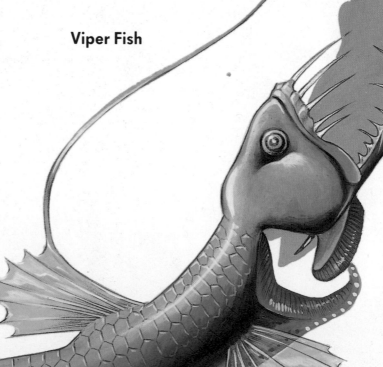

140

A Gulper Eel waits for a meal to swim by ▷

Devils of the dark

Skates, rays and chimaeras are all relatives of sharks. They live as far as 1.5 miles below the ocean's surface. These fish are often compared to devils, because they can produce nasty poisons and powerful electric shocks.

The Atlantic Torpedo Ray feeds on other fish. It stuns its prey with electric shocks produced near the tips of its "wings." Its close relative, the Pacific Big Skate, is equally vicious. Its tail is long and thin and is covered with sharp thorns. When threatened, it whips its tail forward and strikes these against its attacker. One species of chimaera, the Ratfish, has a poisonous spine on top of its head. This can inflict a painful wound.

The Rat-tail Fish uses its sharp spines to warn off predators

The Ancient Greeks and Romans used Electric Rays to try to cure various diseases. They noticed that the fish had unusual effects on the human body, such as making blood clot or relieving headaches. Patients would stand on a Torpedo Ray or have the fish placed on their forehead.

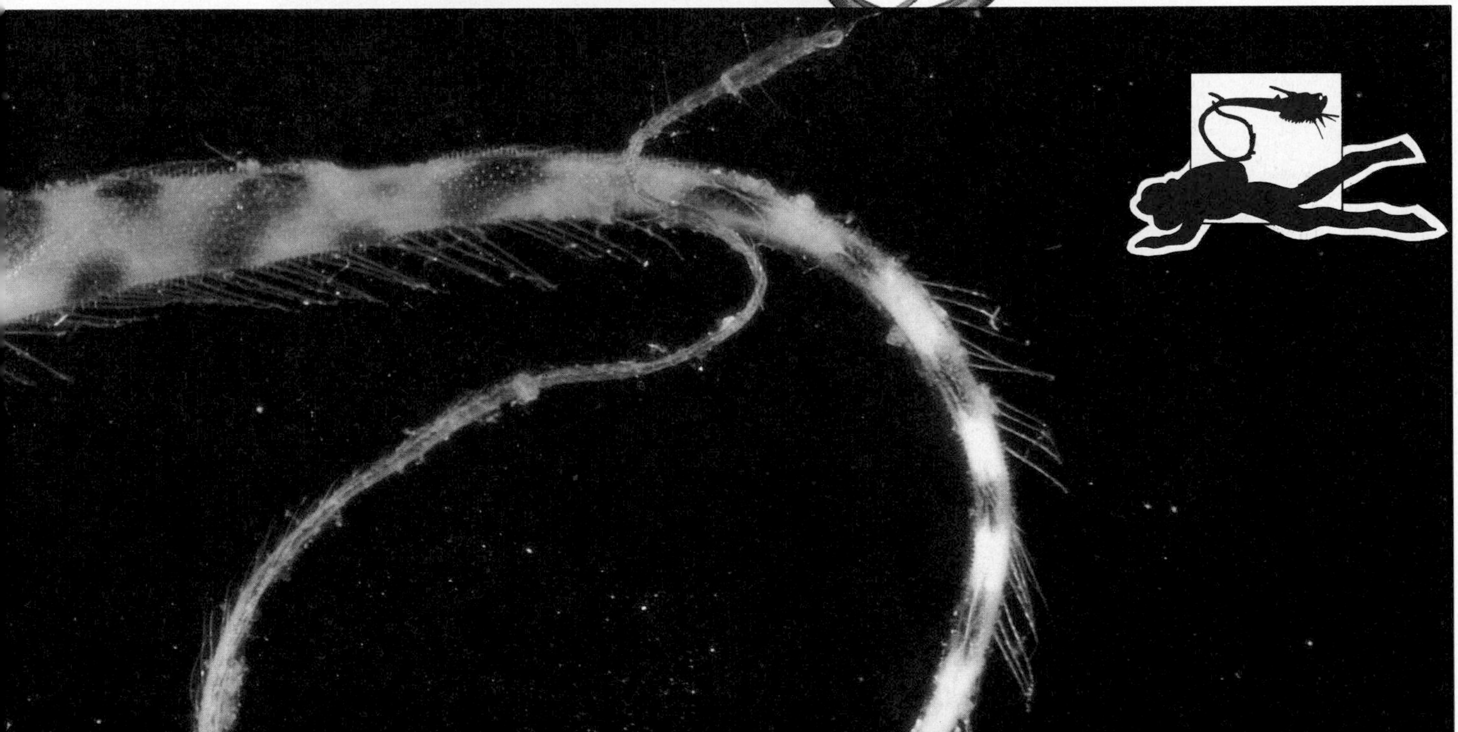

Manta Ray

Eagle Ray

Sting Ray

Angler Fish may produce up to 2 million eggs at a time. These float to the ocean surface in a jelly-like mass. The larvae that hatch from the eggs swim deeper as they grow. Any males that fail to find a female soon die. Once they have bitten into a female, the males will live on her blood.

Three species of Angler Fish

Parasite and host

Some of the strangest deep-sea creatures are the Angler Fish. These tiny predators use a rod and line to catch other fish. The rod is a long and slender fin that grows out of the fish's forehead. At the end of this fin is a lure, like a fisherman's bait. This is often red and shaped like a worm. The lure tempts prey within reach of the Angler's large, teeth-filled jaws.

In some species of Angler Fish, only the females have lures. The males are much smaller than the females. Each one attaches himself to a female and lives on her as a parasite. The male feeds on material from the female's blood system. His only function is to produce sperm to fertilize her eggs.

Two males have attached themselves to this female Angler Fish ▷

Eels

Deep-sea eels grow up to 6 feet long. Like all eels they are predators, with long, thin, tapering bodies and tails. Snipe Eels have slender, flared jaws and file-like teeth. They feed on deep-sea shrimp. These Eels hang upside down in the water and wait for their prey. When a shrimp's legs or antennae get tangled in their jaws, the eels bite their way down the prey until its whole body has been eaten.

Cutthroat Eels have huge mouths, fierce teeth and elastic stomachs. Their teeth angle inwards. This prevents any fish they catch from wriggling free. Another deep-sea eel, the Gulper Eel, has jaws that can grow to a quarter of its body length. It feeds on all kinds of small animals. The Gulper has loose sheets of skin that hang on either side of its mouth. These act like pouches, scooping food into the eel's throat when it opens its jaws.

Eel young, called larvae, look nothing like adult eels. They are transparent and shaped like a leaf or a ribbon. They can take several years to develop into adults. The larvae of most deep-sea eels live and feed close to the surface.

Gulper Eel with prey

The Snipe Eel grows to 1 foot long ▷

Deep divers

Male Sperm Whales are believed to dive 1.8 miles or more under the sea. They use their strong tails to swim steadily downwards into the dark, cold waters. Sometimes the whales move along the ocean floor and plow the mud for food. Usually, though, they stay still in the water and wait in ambush for squid. The Sperm Whale can stay underwater for up to 90 minutes before having to come to the surface to breathe.

The Leatherback Turtle can go for an even longer time without air—possibly up to 20 hours. But it doesn't dive as deep. This sea turtle feeds on jellyfish, snails and other soft-bodied animals. It can grow to 9 feet long and can swim very fast—up to 19mph.

A Sperm Whale swims along near the surface △

Nautiluses are close relatives of squid and octopuses. They have a hard outer shell. They use their tentacles, which are covered in suckers, to catch fish.

Giant Squid

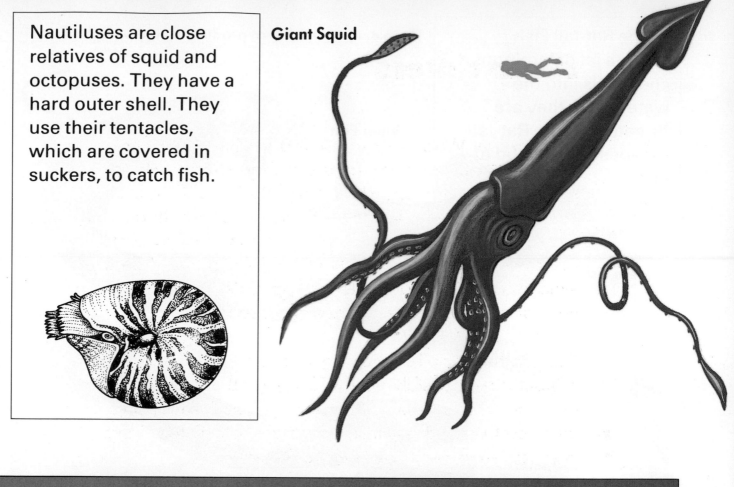

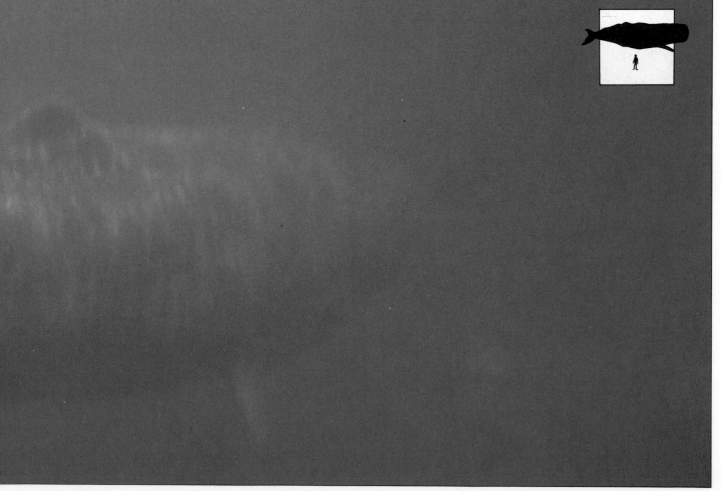

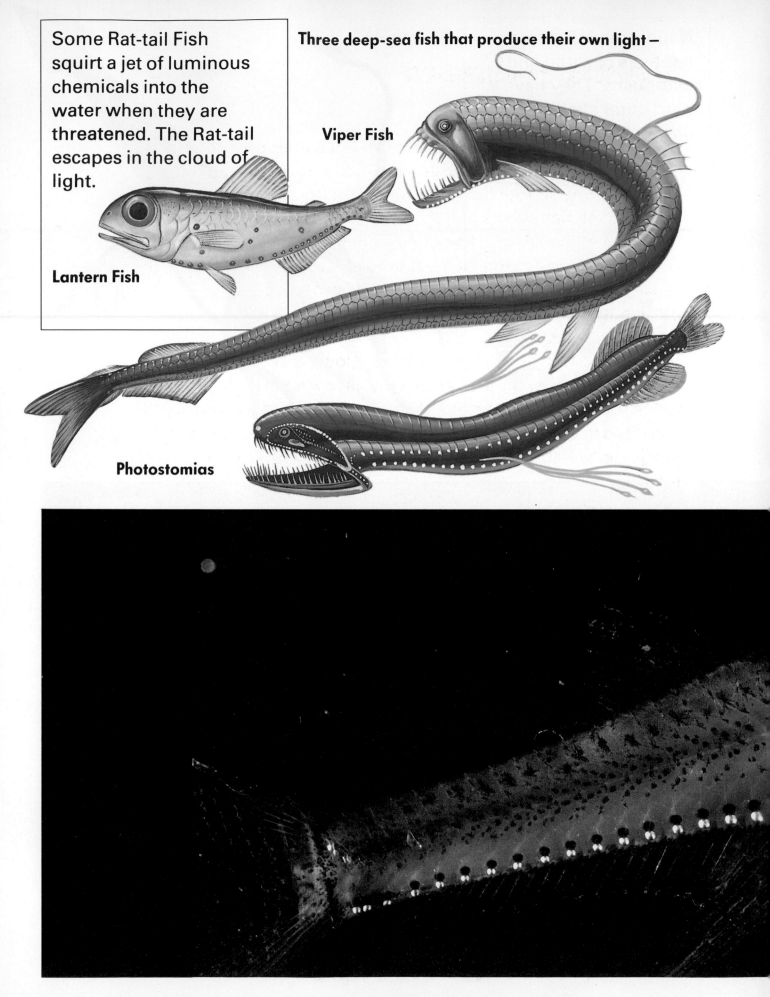

Some Rat-tail Fish squirt a jet of luminous chemicals into the water when they are threatened. The Rat-tail escapes in the cloud of light.

Lantern Fish

Three deep-sea fish that produce their own light –

Viper Fish

Photostomias

150   **Lantern Fish have rows of lights that look like portholes on a boat** △

Light-producers

Hundreds of species of deep-sea fish have their own "flashlights" – structures that glow in the dark. They use these to hunt for food or to find mates in the darkness. Lantern fish have rows of light-producing organs down the sides of their body. The glow from these organs probably disguises the fish's outline as it swims towards the surface to feed. Other lights on its body are used to attract mates.

Some species of Dragon Fish have glowing bulbs which they use as lures, in the same way that Angler Fish do. Other deep-sea fish have light organs positioned next to their eyes. These emit a red light to which their eyes are highly sensitive. They may act as searchlights to hunt for prey.

On the ocean bed

Many deep-sea creatures live buried in the mud on the ocean floor. Ragworms make burrows for protection, though they often come out to scavenge for food. Beard Worms live in long tubes that protrude from the mud. Only their head parts are exposed. The head bears up to 250 long threads, or tentacles. These are probably used both to gather food particles from the water and as gills for breathing.

Giant Tube Worms have long tentacles that they use in the same way. They live around volcanic hot water and sulfur "chimneys" that are found far below the surface. Inside the worms' bodies are bacteria that can convert sulfur substances into energy. This energy is used by both the bacteria and the worms. No other animal known to man produces energy in this way.

Beard Worm　　　　**Worm with many tentacles**

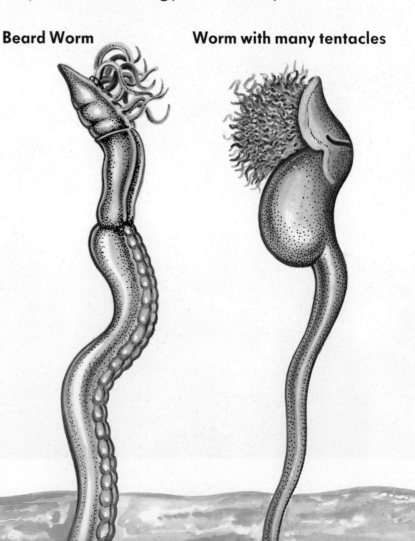

Tripod Fish live as far as 4.8 miles under the sea. They rest on the ocean floor on their stiff lower fins and their tails. They feed on any shellfish that drift past.

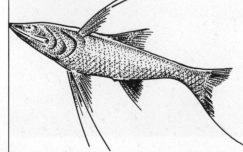

Starfish and Sea Lilies

A whole family of spiny-skinned animals lives and hunts on the ocean floor. The best-known members are Starfish. They have a flattened body and five or more spreading arms. On the underside of each arm are "tube-feet," like the suckers of an octopus. Starfish feed on clams, oysters and mussels. They use their tube-feet to pry open the shells of these animals and to pass the flesh toward the central mouth.

Sea Cucumbers also have tube-feet. These are arranged in a ring around the mouth, which is at one end of their sack-like body. Some species trap pieces of food with their tube-feet. Others swallow sand and mud from the ocean floor. Sea Lilies use their branching arms to strain food from the water.

The tube-feet of Starfish are arranged in rows on the arms. They use water to produce a sucking action.

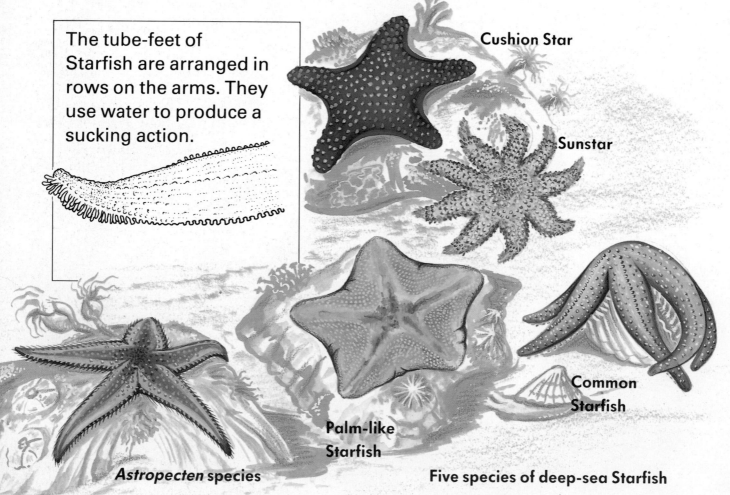

Cushion Star

Sunstar

Common Starfish

Palm-like Starfish

Astropecten species

Five species of deep-sea Starfish

154

Survival File

The seas and oceans of the world are enormous. Until recently people thought of them as a never-ending source of food – fish, shellfish and whales – and as a convenient dumping ground for waste. But fish populations cannot survive if too many fish are caught year after year. This overfishing also upsets the populations of plants and other animals in the oceans. The dumping of harmful chemicals and sewage into the water pollutes oceans, harming all forms of life. Even the greatest depths are now threatened.

Oil spills harm ocean life at all depths

In the last 20 years or so, special underwater craft known as submersibles and new photographic techniques have been developed. These have allowed us to explore the ocean's depths for the first time. Submersibles can go down to 16,500 feet, and recording instruments can be sent down to the ocean floor and brought back to the surface. Together, these have greatly increased our knowlege of creatures of the deep.

Many species of shark are overfished
Occasionally, fishing boats catch and haul up fish that normally live in deep waters. But many deep-sea fish have air-filled bags to help them float. When they are brought to the surface the bags expand. The fish literally explode and die the instant they are taken from the water. But even from the remains, scientists are finding that these fish may be useful sources of food and of chemicals that can combat diseases.

Nuclear debris on a Pacific island
Protecting deep-sea creatures, and indeed all ocean life, is therefore important. Nowadays, most nations of the world have agreed to restrict fishing and the dumping of hazardous materials. But oil spills and illegal dumping of waste from factories and nuclear power stations still goes on. Pesticides sprayed onto the land end up in the sea. Unless we clean up our act, many deep-sea creatures will become extinct before we can find out much about them and how they live.

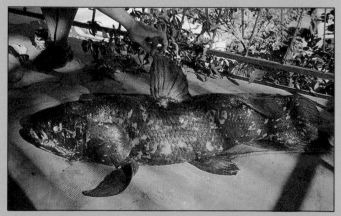

The Coelacanth, a deep-sea "living fossil"

Identification Chart

This chart shows you some of the creatures that live in the ocean depths. Most of these creatures are difficult to see. To do this, you will have to visit a marine park or large aquarium, though sometimes they are hauled up by fishing boats and may be part of the catch brought ashore. Each square of the grid represents 4 inches.

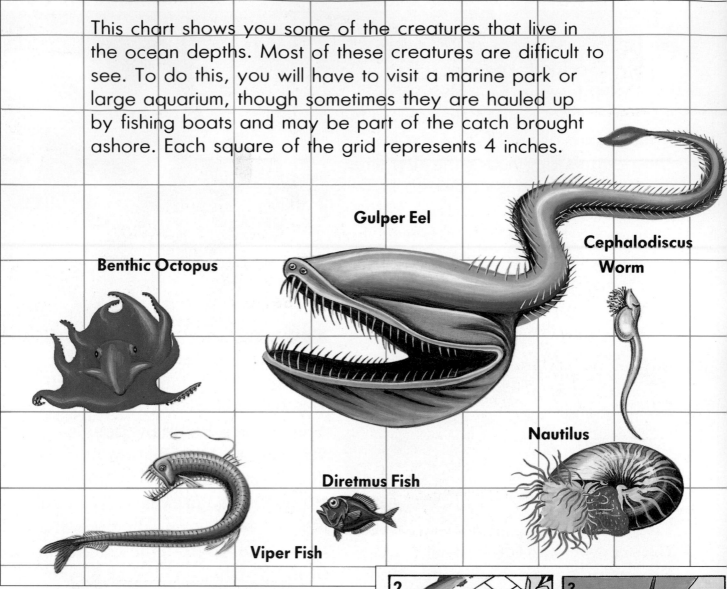

Gulper Eel

Benthic Octopus

Cephalodiscus Worm

Nautilus

Diretmus Fish

Viper Fish

Make your own deep-sea world

1. Using the chart above, draw the outlines of some deep-sea fish on a sheet of tracing paper.

2,3. With a black felt-tip pen and paintbrush, fill in the shapes but leave the light-producing organs white.

4. Paint around the silhouettes with a dark paint that will block the light.

5. Using cardboard supports, stand the sheet in front of a light and make the luminous organs glow.

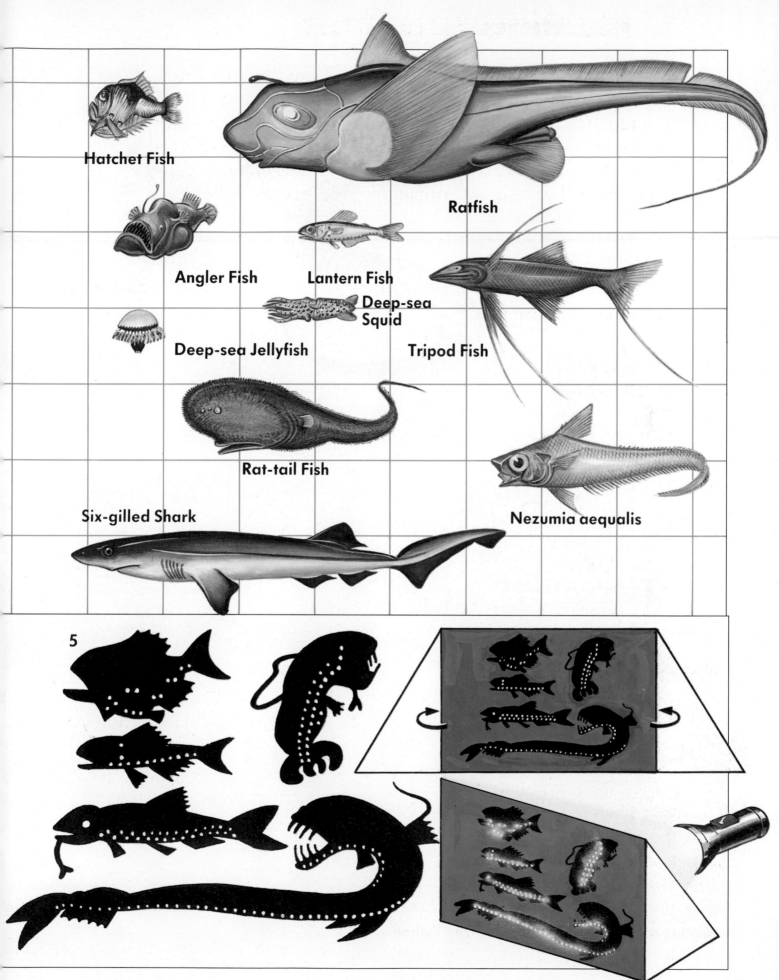

Hatchet Fish

Ratfish

Angler Fish

Lantern Fish

Deep-sea Squid

Deep-sea Jellyfish

Tripod Fish

Rat-tail Fish

Six-gilled Shark

Nezumia aequalis

5

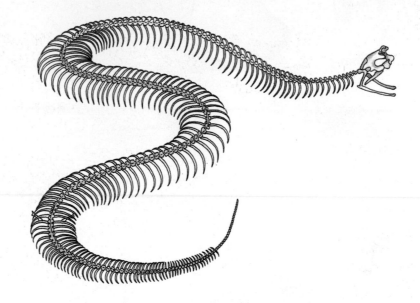

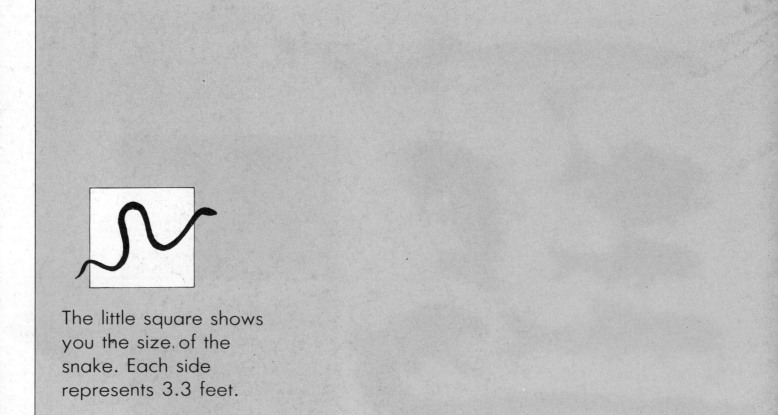

The little square shows you the size of the snake. Each side represents 3.3 feet.

The picture opposite shows a Green Tree Python

Chapter 6
PYTHONS
AND
BOAS

Lionel Bender

Facts to Know

Pythons and boas were the first types of snake to evolve on Earth more than 70 million years ago. They lack the venom, or poison, of some of the more highly evolved snakes. But with their large, stout bodies they are strong and efficient hunters. Nearly 75 kinds are known and they live in many different habitats in the warmer parts of the world.

Pythons and boas include some of the biggest living reptiles. They can grow to lengths of 23 feet or more. Some species are quite common, although many are becoming rare. Several kinds are seldom seen because of their secretive habits. In the ways they move and the senses they use, pythons and boas are unique in the animal world.

◁ **D'Albert's Python**

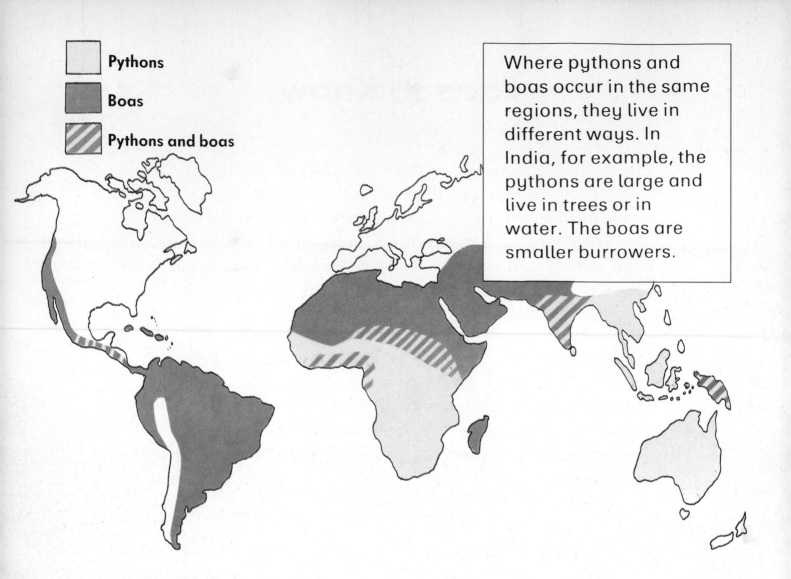

Pythons

Boas

Pythons and boas

Where pythons and boas occur in the same regions, they live in different ways. In India, for example, the pythons are large and live in trees or in water. The boas are smaller burrowers.

Telling boas from pythons

At first glance pythons and boas seem very similar. Many of them are large snakes and they all kill by constriction. This means they coil their body around their victim and squeeze it until it suffocates. Unlike most other snakes they have tiny traces of hind limbs. They also have two fully developed lungs instead of the usual single snake lung.

However, there are some important differences between boas and pythons. Pythons have teeth on the front bone of the upper jaw whereas boas do not. There are also small differences in the shape and size of skull bones. And pythons lay eggs while boas produce live young.

The Carpet Python lives in Australia and New Guinea ▷

Eggs and babies

Pythons lay between 10 and 100 eggs. One Indian python is known to have laid 107. The eggs must be kept warm if they are to hatch. They are left in a nest of rotting vegetation, which acts as an incubator. Asian pythons curl around their eggs and this keeps them warmer than the surroundings.

When hatching, the baby snake slashes a hole in the parchment-like shell with its sharp egg-tooth. The tooth, which points forward from its top gum, is lost soon after the baby crawls out. Boas keep their eggs in the body and the young are born live. The young snakes are able to look after themselves right away and grow fast. A python may be 29 inches long on hatching and up to 6.6 feet a year later.

An Anaconda with newly born young

A Reticulated Python curled around its eggs ▷

Snake skeletons

The skeleton of a snake needs to be both strong and flexible. So snakes have a large number of vertebrae—the bones that make up the backbone—with only a small amount of bending between each one. All vertebrae, except those of the neck region, have ribs. In the tail region the ribs are fused to the backbone.

Boas and pythons also have a tiny set of hip bones. The hips are not attached to the backbone. There are even tiny traces of back legs. These end in claws that can just be seen on the outside of the body. The skull, like that of other snakes, is built for swallowing large items of food. The jawbones are loosely attached to one another by elastic ligaments so that the mouth can be opened extremely wide.

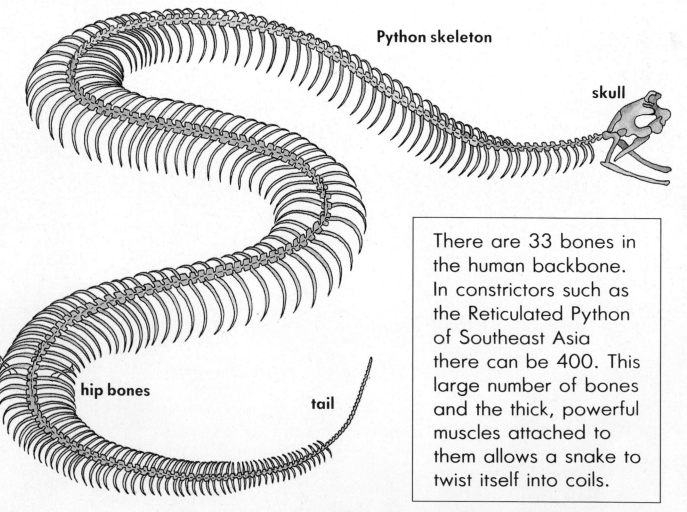

Python skeleton

skull

hip bones

tail

There are 33 bones in the human backbone. In constrictors such as the Reticulated Python of Southeast Asia there can be 400. This large number of bones and the thick, powerful muscles attached to them allows a snake to twist itself into coils.

The Anaconda can wrap its body around its prey in tight coils ▷

The heat sensors of snakes are found in no other backboned animal. They allow the snake to find and strike at prey even in the dark.

eye with spectacle

heat-sensing pits

sense organs in head detect vibrations

Jacobson's organ in roof of mouth

tongue

Senses

A snake cannot hear sounds in the air as we do. But using sense organs within its skull, it can detect vibrations in the ground. Snakes do not have eyelids. Instead each eye is protected by a transparent covering, the spectacle. Their sight is rather poor.

The tongue plays an important part in a snake's senses. An organ in the roof of the mouth, Jacobson's organ, is sensitive to chemicals. The snake uses its forked tongue to gather chemicals from the ground or air and places them in Jacobson's organ. The snake can "taste" or "smell" a scent trail using this sense. Some snakes can also sense the body heat of their prey through heat sensors called pits.

The New Guinea Tree-python has large heat-sensitive pits on its lip ▷

Catching food

As they do not have poison fangs, pythons and boas rely on speed and strength to catch prey. They lie in wait, often anchoring the rear part of their body to a tree. When prey comes within range they strike fast and grip it with their sharp teeth. Then they wrap their body around and around the victim and hold on tight. When the prey breathes out, the snake tightens its hold and stops it from breathing in again. The prey soon suffocates. Then the snake swallows its victim whole.

Many of the animals caught by constricting snakes are quite small, like rats, mice, birds and frogs. But large African pythons can take small deer and antelopes. Once constricting snakes grow to more than 10 feet long they are strong enough to be a threat to all but the largest wildlife. There are even recorded instances of Asian pythons catching and eating small children. However, it is unlikely that they could swallow an adult.

A Rock Python strikes and overpowers its prey

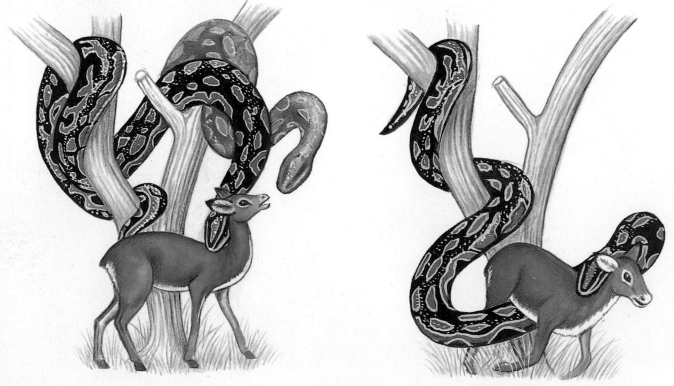

172

An African Rock Python catches 44-pound Thomson's Gazelle

One African python is known to have captured and eaten a leopard. Another ate a jackal at each of three meals. A 10-foot-long South American boa caught and ate an ocelot.

Feasting and fasting

Once a constrictor snake has killed an animal, it sets about swallowing it. First it uses its teeth to get a good grip on the prey. The teeth are pointed and curve backwards, which prevents the victims from wriggling free from the snake's jaws. Snakes have extremely mobile jawbones, which can swing outwards and slightly apart. The lower jawbones can move forward along the prey's body to drag it into the snake's mouth. With their stretchable throat skin, a python or boa can swallow an animal that is much wider than its own head.

It may take 30 minutes to completely swallow a large prey. It can remain visible inside the snake's body for several days. Gradually, the snake's digestive juices dissolve it away. Snakes are cold-blooded and do not need to burn up food to keep warm, so they do not need to eat very often. In the course of a year, a python may eat no more than its own weight in food.

The Rock Python swallows its prey

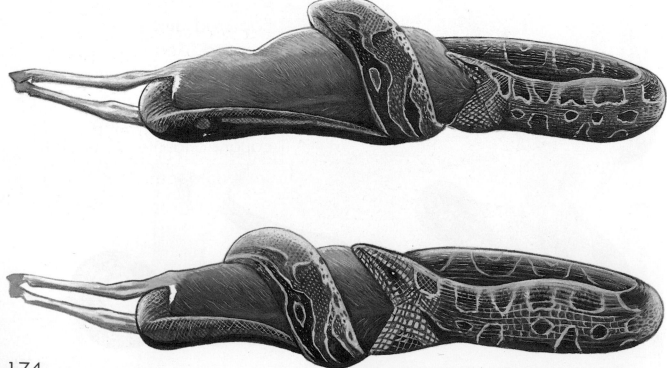

174

A wallaby meal distends the body of a Scrub Python

A South American boa has been known to survive for 16 months without a meal. Apart from becoming thinner – it lost half its body weight – the snake did not seem to suffer. It eventually began feeding again.

The stripes of Boelen's Python break up its outline

Defense

When cornered by an enemy like a big cat, pythons and boas defend themselves by striking and biting. They rarely try to constrict attackers. The small sand boas are amongst the fiercest defenders, delivering slashing sideways bites.

Many constrictors are protected by their skin color. Several tree pythons are green like leaves, and scrub pythons have blotches that disguise the outline of their bodies. Snakes also keep still for much of the time, which makes them difficult to see. The Rubber Boa of North America protects itself by rolling into a ball. Its head stays safe within the ball while it waves its tail about like a threatening head.

The Ball Python, true to its name, rolls up for protection ▷

In the trees

The Emerald Tree Boa of South America is fully adapted to living in trees. It has a strong tail able to grip branches. Its beautiful green coloring and white markings give good camouflage against the leafy background. At rest it balances its coils neatly over a branch. It has long front teeth that help it seize its prey—mainly birds—at the first attempt.

On the other side of the world, the New Guinea Tree Python has the same coloring and adaptations for life in the trees. Many of the constricting snakes can climb if they have to, for example to avoid an attacker. Some, like the tree boas, spend nearly all the time in trees, hunting mainly at night and resting in the shade during the day.

The Marbled Tree Boa

The Emerald Tree Boa is agile enough to catch birds and squirrels ▷

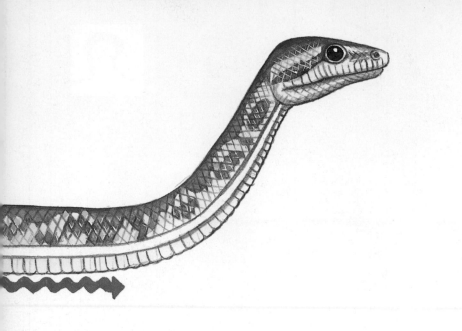

Python moving in "rectilinear," or straight-line, fashion

On the ground

Pythons and boas seldom use the side-to-side
wriggling action we normally associate with snakes.
These heavy-bodied snakes normally move by
crawling slowly in a straight line. They use the wide,
flat skin scales that run across the belly to dig into the
ground and pull themselves along. Sections of the
body are moved forward and then lowered to the
ground to grip. The snake can climb up steep slopes
and stalk up on prey with a minimum of effort.

Climbing constrictors sometimes move using a
concertina-like action. When the front part of the body
is able to grip a support, the snake then folds up its tail
and back part and pulls them forward.

180   **A Kenyan Sand Boa shows the typical snake side-to-side body movement ▷**

Swamps and deserts

Water is an attractive habitat to large pythons and boas. It helps support their heavy bodies. They can swim well, moving through the water like fish. The big snake most closely associated with water is the South American Anaconda. It spends most of its time in the water, often close to the edge of a swamp or river. It swims slowly with nostrils and eyes above the surface, ready to seize prey.

The sand boas of West Asia and North Africa are just as at home in dry grasslands or deserts. They are small snakes with a head no wider than their body. The tail is short and blunt. They have tiny scales, small eyes, and appear to swim through the sand.

Mexican Burrowing Python

A number of small boas burrow in leaf litter and damp soil. These include the Mexican Burrowing Python and the Calabar Ground Python of West African forests, which is often found in termite nests.

A Rock Python is at home in the water, but must surface to breathe ▷

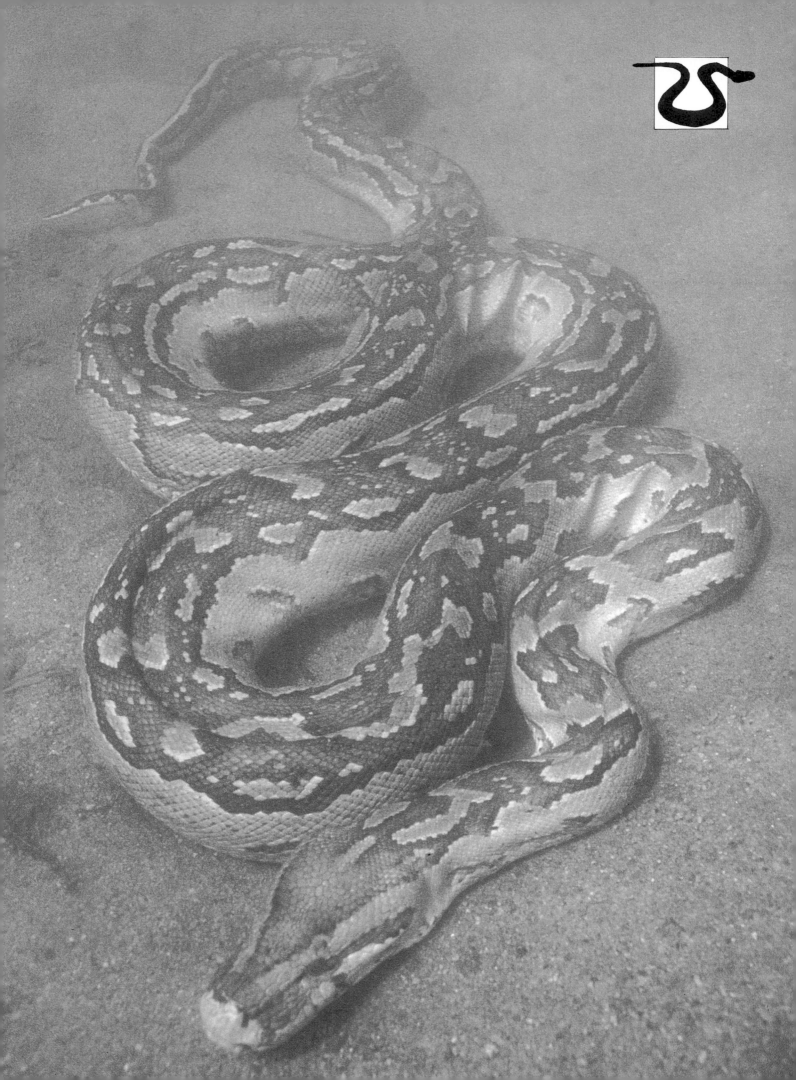

Giants among giants

Snakes can live for up to 40 years and they continue growing even when adult. In order to grow, snakes shed the horny layer of skin that covers their scales. Young snakes can shed their skin six or seven times a year. The real giants among snakes are probably very old snakes living in favorable conditions.

The longest snake on record was 33 feet long, a Reticulated Python in the Philippines. But the biggest snake of all is probably the South American Anaconda. The longest that has been reliably measured was only 27.7 feet. However, many people believe it may grow to over 36 feet. It is certainly the heaviest snake. Large individuals weigh around 440 pounds.

A Boa Constrictor after shedding its skin

The Reticulated Python of Southeast Asia is the longest of all snakes ▷

Survival file

In spite of the size and power of some of the big constrictors, there are few recorded cases of them killing or eating humans. On the other hand, many pythons and boas are killed by people — for food, for skins, or indirectly by the spoiling of the places where they live. Like many animals, they and their habitat are threatened by human activities.

A python is often part of a snake charmer's show

In many parts of Asia and Africa python meat is a welcome addition to the human diet. These snakes are said to be tasty. Many pythons are killed to provide snakeskin leather to make handbags or shoes. In years when snakeskin has been very fashionable, millions of snakes have been killed.

Another "use" to which the big pythons and boas are put is in snake charming. Most of these snakes are even-tempered and soon become used to handling. They make dramatic props for snake charmers or people in other branches of show business. If they are too lively they can be quieted by cooling them with water or cold air.

Snakeskins may be sold as souvenirs

The greatest threat to the big snakes today lies in the way people treat their habitat. As the tropical forests are cut down, the places in which animals like Emerald Tree Boas can live become fewer.

In the West Indies some small species of boas are becoming rare because of human activity. On Round Island in the Indian Ocean there are two species of boas. Once they were also found on nearby Mauritius. But they were exterminated, along with the Dodo, by people and their animals. Without care many kinds of big snake could disappear.

Much of the Amazon forest is being cleared

Identification chart

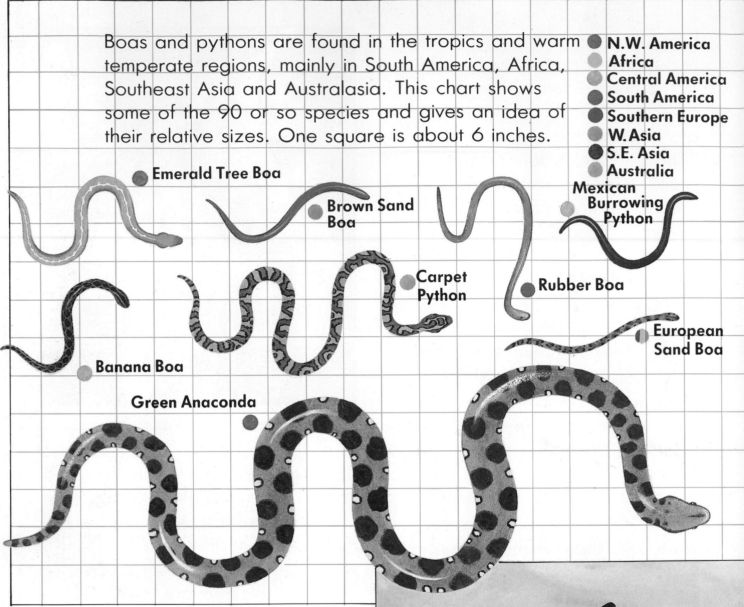

Boas and pythons are found in the tropics and warm temperate regions, mainly in South America, Africa, Southeast Asia and Australasia. This chart shows some of the 90 or so species and gives an idea of their relative sizes. One square is about 6 inches.

- N.W. America
- Africa
- Central America
- South America
- Southern Europe
- W. Asia
- S.E. Asia
- Australia

Emerald Tree Boa

Brown Sand Boa

Mexican Burrowing Python

Carpet Python

Rubber Boa

European Sand Boa

Banana Boa

Green Anaconda

Making a twisting python

1. Mark out cutting area as shown on several cardboard rolls.

2. Color each section using one of the snakes above for reference.
3. Cut out each roll as shown.
4. Cut out and color head. Use paper or ribbon for the tongue.
5. Join each section together with wire or clips.
6. Hold snake at end and twist slightly to make it wriggle.

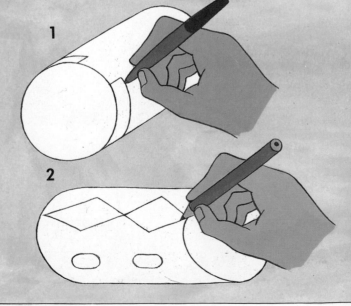

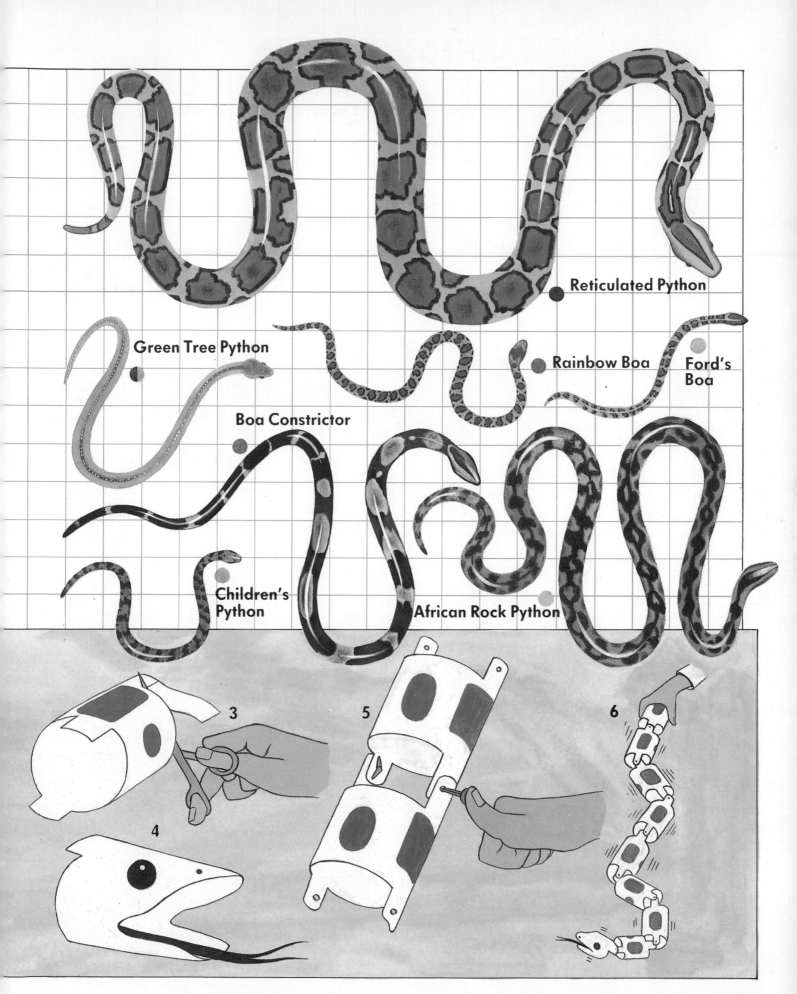

Reticulated Python

Green Tree Python

Rainbow Boa

Ford's Boa

Boa Constrictor

Children's Python

African Rock Python

3

4

5

6